EASY GERMAN COOKBOOK

EASY GERMAN COOKBOOK

80 Classic Recipes Made Simple

Karen Lodder

Photography by Marija Vidal

callisto
publishing
an imprint of Sourcebooks

Copyright © 2021 by Callisto Publishing LLC
Cover and internal design © 2021 by Callisto Publishing LLC
Photography © 2021 Marija Vidal, food styling by Victoria Woollard
Author photo courtesy of Kevin Rockwell
Interior and Cover Designer: Jill Lee
Art Producer: Hannah Dickerson
Editors: Justin Hartung, Sierra Machado
Production Editor: Ruth Sakata Corley
Production Manager: Michael Kay

Callisto and the colophon are registered trademarks of Callisto Publishing LLC.

Published by Callisto Publishing LLC C/O Sourcebooks LLC
P.O. Box 4410, Naperville, Illinois 60567-4410
(630) 961-3900
callistopublishing.com
Printed in the United States of America
VP 2

For Dana, Katy, Stephen, and especially Kevin, who ate almost everything I put in front of them, and for Bella, who ate the rest.

CONTENTS

INTRODUCTION

My parents immigrated to California just before I was born, and because my mother knew how to cook German food, that's what we ate. (Of course, to us, she just prepared food.) When we visited German relatives, the same foods arrived on the table: roast pork with red cabbage, schnitzel and fried potatoes, and didn't everyone eat a Christmas goose? Since many of our family friends were German immigrants as well, serving bratwurst at a barbecue seemed perfectly normal. Not until I grew up and ate at other tables outside of my childhood bubble did I realize how "different" our meals were and how they looked from the outside. There were more than a few times when I put an old favorite dish on the table and got a "what's this?" look from friends. (To be fair, I thought herring salad deserved that look myself.)

But one bite and they were converted.

German food is flavorful and satisfying. When moist medallions of pork tenderloin with mushroom sauce or a spicy goulash soup come to the table, there are "mmms" and requests for the recipe. And, as I like to point out to my foodie friends, Germans were eating kale before kale was cool. They just transformed it into a delicious one-pot meal with sausage and potatoes. (My Oma would be wildly confused at the thought of a kale smoothie!)

A recent poll shows that one in five Americans can claim some German ancestry, and German festivals and Oktoberfests are springing up around the country, creating new interest in German foods. Whether our families arrived with the 48ers (that's 1848!) or flew over on a 747, deep inside we crave the homey food our *Omas* (grandmothers) cooked. Still, learning to cook German food may seem a little daunting, even for those who had German grandmothers. A pinch of this and a spoonful of that, and suddenly, a delicious meal appears! It can feel like a magic trick, and the secrets weren't always written down.

Over the years I've been working on cracking those secrets, making the traditional foods more accessible. That's why these 80 easy recipes are made with ingredients generally found in American supermarkets. I've also made sure to include appropriate substitutions and work-arounds for hard-to-find items. (Honestly, why is Quark so hard to find?) My Oma didn't have a lot of fancy kitchen gadgets, and you won't need them, either.

As a working parent, I'm also mindful of time (and energy). There are plenty of quick 30-minute recipes or recipes that you just need to get started and can then leave alone to cook themselves. German *Eintöpfe* are the one-pot wonders that everyone needs in their life, so I included a few favorites. Naturally, there are great ideas for *Brotzeit* or *Abendbrot*, the German tradition of serving bread with cold cuts, cheeses, spreads, and vegetables as a complete meal.

My hope is that this *Easy German Cookbook* will shatter a few stereotypes and allow you to enjoy traditional German foods . . . and maybe someday you, too, will just think of them as food.

CHAPTER 1

GERMAN FAVORITES MADE SIMPLE

When asked to describe German food, most people will immediately mention Oktoberfest specialties such as sausages, pretzels, and Black Forest cake, plus giant steins of beer being drunk by a guy wearing Lederhosen. And while those foods (and the Lederhosen guy) exist in Germany, they are certainly not the country's whole culinary story. Germany's different states and regions, much like those in the United States, specialize in different foods that are influenced by local products and history. In this chapter, you'll learn about those differences and get advice on stocking your kitchen to make this book's easy adaptations of German favorites.

The Culture and Cuisine

If my Oma were alive to hear culinary buzzwords like "seasonal cooking" and "snout-to-tail cuisine," she probably would laugh. German food has always been seasonal and tied to the harvest (as anyone who's witnessed white asparagus season mania knows). If you could eat it, my Oma could make a delicious and satisfying meal out of it (although, thankfully, some of her specialties, like brains, have dropped off the menu).

Home cooking in Germany follows the rhythm of the seasons. Vegetables from the garden or farmers' market show up on the table to accompany the main dish, or they end up in filling *Eintöpfe* (one-pot meals). Fruits take center stage for *Nachtisch* (dessert), whether eaten fresh or stewed into a compote and served over pudding. Meals generally spotlight meat, in the form of a roast or chop, and a gravy or sauce will stretch that flavor across ever-present potatoes.

Germans traditionally eat their warm, cooked, heavy meal at midday instead of in the evening. To me that makes perfect sense: A solid *Mittagessen* (midday meal) gives you the fuel you need to get through the rest of the day. Then, instead of cooking at the end of the day, most Germans round out the meal schedule with *Abendbrot* (also called *Vespers*), a plate of bread, butter, cheese, and cold cuts, sometimes accompanied by a side of pickles, sliced radishes, or fresh tomatoes.

On Sundays, my mother and Oma would take extra care when tying an apron over their nice dresses before cooking. Sunday dinners would usually have several courses that took hours to prepare. And special holiday meals on Christmas and Easter took even more preparation because of all the courses, starting with soup, followed by a pork, beef, or game roast (or even a whole cooked goose), accompanied by handmade dumplings, vegetables, and salad, and pudding for dessert. After eating, we'd all fall into a food coma and then take a family walk to help digestion. The oven would barely cool off before it was time for coffee and cake.

Regional Cuisine

Germany's culinary regions mostly align with its states. Each region specializes in dishes that make the most of what grows there, and in some cases, there are influences from neighboring countries. Rye and barley from the acidic soils of the East are used to make hearty breads and stews. The lush hillsides of Bavaria are perfect for dairy farming and cheese. And nowhere in the world will you find better conditions for growing hops, an essential component of beer, than in the Hallertau. The northern part of Germany touches on the North Sea and the Baltic, so seafood is commonly found on menus in the North.

Naturally, the different corners of the country have dishes that are mostly enjoyed in that region. *Fischbrötchen*, a bread roll with pickled herring, is a common grab-and-go meal all over Hamburg, because of its connection to the North Sea, but you would be hard-pressed to find it in Munich. The *Weisswurstäquator* (white sausage equator) divides Germany, meaning *Weißwurst*, a simmered white sausage, is favored to the south in Bavaria. Far north of that line, in Berlin, they prefer *Currywurst,* grilled bratwurst smothered in a curry-laced ketchup. *Sauerbraten*, a beef roast that spends days marinating in a mixture of vinegar, red wine, and juniper berries, got its start in the Rhineland's cattle country, then spread across the country and even traveled to America with early emigrants. In the northeastern state of Brandenburg, they love their *Königsberger Klopse*, a dish of meatballs in white caper sauce named for Königsberg, the original capital of Prussia.

Some German foods came from parts of Europe that were once part of the country. Silesia may no longer be part of Germany (today it's in Poland), but its food legacy lives on. Silesian cooking incorporates a lot of fruit in main dishes and poppy seeds in cake, and it's the origin of everyone's favorite German meal, *Rouladen*, thin, flat pieces of beef that are topped with mustard, onion, pickles, and bacon, then rolled up before braising. And the original *Goulaschsuppe* (goulash soup), heavily flavored with paprika, came from Germans in Hungary.

Probably the most obvious example of regional differences can be found in the simple side dish potato salad. In fact, the best way to start a fight in Germany is to claim that you have the best recipe for potato salad. Every part of Germany makes the dish their own way: hot or cold; using mayo, stock, or vinegar; with or without bacon or apple. (For the record, my family is in the mayo and apple camp.) Additionally, every German Oma has her own variation. You could say Germany is a nation divided by potato salad. I've included both hot and cold recipes in this book, so everyone should be satisfied.

Although a side dish may drive people apart, bread brings everyone back together. Bread is everything in Germany, and with more than 300 varieties of bread and 1,200 different types of rolls, it's no wonder that German bread has achieved UNESCO Intangible Cultural Heritage status. Although every region has a different name for bread rolls: *Semmel* in the Southeast, *Weck* in the Southwest, and *Schrippe* in Berlin, most Germans will happily consume a *Brötchen* (crusty bread roll) for breakfast, no matter what part of Germany they live in.

Different states with similar language and background all melted together into this wonderful place my family called home. Here are some of the hallmarks of Germany's main culinary regions, plus some recipes from each that you'll find in this book.

SOUTHWEST (BADEN, SAARLAND, SWABIA)

An ideal growing climate and proximity to France's food culture give Southwest Germany a rich culinary heritage. If you love fine dining, you will find the most Michelin stars in this corner of the country. But that love for food also turns up at home, where simple, fresh ingredients become tasty meals. Famous foods from this region include Potato Dumplings (page 37), German Egg Noodles (page 35), and Filled German Dumplings (page 67). And, most famously, Black Forest Cherry Cake (page 126).

BAVARIA AND FRANCONIA

Although Bavaria and Franconia are officially one state, the Franconians like to make sure you know it was not always that way. Still, one thing they do agree on is beer. Upper Franconia may have the highest density of breweries per capita, but Bavarian breweries produce more beer. And beer is considered a food in Bavaria! Thanks to Oktoberfest, this is the corner of Germany whose food most people are familiar with. Roasted Pork Hocks (page 76), German Soft Pretzels (page 28), Roast Chicken (page 48), and breaded pork schnitzel may have originated in Austria, but the Bavarians can't get enough of them. Still, there are divisions. Although the Bavarians adore their poached *Weißwurst* sausage, the Franconians happily munch on the short Nürnberger bratwurst.

NORTHWEST (LOWER SAXONY, BREMEN, HAMBURG, SCHLESWIG-HOLSTEIN, MECKLENBURG–WESTERN POMERANIA)

In Northern Germany, you'll find seafood on the menu, including *Fisch-brötchen* (fish rolls), Herring Salad (page 114), and delicious smoked fish. But its proximity to cold sea air means the region also favors warm and hearty foods. Locals plan hikes around certain restaurants to enjoy Kale Soup with Sausage (page 80). Corned Beef Hash with Beets (page 95), another regional favorite, originated on sailing ships, because the meat could be transported without spoiling. And of course, we can thank the people of Hamburg for giving us the hamburger, although the original recipe for German Beef Patties (page 84), known in Germany as *Frikadellen*, is often served without a bun.

RHINELAND AND WESTPHALIA

North Rhine–Westphalia, where my family lives, is farm country, so the diet seems hearty to outsiders. Substantial soups made with peas or lentils and loaded with sausage, Pan-Fried Trout (page 110), and crispy Potato Pancakes (page 38) are local favorites. Other areas may serve Marinated Roast Beef (page 92), but the original comes from the Rhineland.

NORTHEAST (BERLIN, BRANDENBURG)

Berlin has always been a place of cultural diversity, which makes Berliners happy to try new things, like Bratwurst with Curry Sauce (page 66). Since Berlin is surrounded by Brandenburg, Berliners have access to the amazing produce from that state, especially cucumbers and fruit, the basis for *Kaltschale* (cold fruit soup) and Red Berry Pudding (page 118). Frederick the Great planted the first potatoes in Potsdam, just south of Berlin, and in a very short time he changed the German kitchen. And Prussian Meatballs in White Caper Sauce (page 86), which the Germans call *Königsberger Klopse* for the old capital of Prussia, are still enormously popular.

EAST (THURINGIA, SAXONY-ANHALT)

Thuringia and Saxony-Anhalt, once part of East Germany, are known for amazing produce and beef. Asparagus and root vegetables are on the menu in this area, which was once world renowned for its incredible selection of seed varieties. Home chefs make Frankish Beef Roast with Onion Sauce (page 94) and *Würzfleisch* (a cheese-topped casserole of meat and vegetables), all washed down with wine (often sparkling) produced in the northernmost wine region in Germany.

THE BEST OF THE WURSTS

Germany produces 1,500 different kinds of sausages that can turn up at any meal or as a snack. Smoked, steamed, boiled, or grilled, they can be served whole or sliced. The recipes in this book all use easy-to-source sausages that can be found in your local grocery store.

Bratwurst: Made from coarsely ground pork or beef combined with spices, these sausages get grilled or pan-fried. You can serve them in rolls, with mustard, or with curry sauce.

Smoked sausages: Made from pork or beef with a lot of seasonings, smoked sausages are hearty and flavorful. They turn up in soups or stews, and some, like *Landjäger* or salami, are sliced and eaten as a snack or with bread.

Wieners or frankfurters: Wieners look the most like a hot dog, but these special, lightly smoked sausages have more of a "snap" when you bite into them. Serve them with potato salad for a complete meal.

Your German Kitchen

My mother had no problems putting authentic German food on our California table, and these days it's even easier. Most German cooking can be easily reproduced with ingredients found in your local supermarket or farmers' markets.

Fresh Produce and Herbs

CABBAGE: Cabbage, both red and green varieties, turns up everywhere in German recipes, in side dishes, in salads, and as wrappers for cabbage rolls.

FRESH HERBS: With a refrigerator (or even better, a container garden) full of fresh dill, parsley, thyme, and especially chives, you should be able to satisfy most of your fresh herb requirements. Plus, a sprinkle of chopped chives or parsley on any finished dish just makes it look super professional.

GREEN BEANS: Green beans are my favorite vegetable, and here you'll find them as a side dish and as the main ingredient in hearty and delicious Green Bean Soup (page 102).

KALE: I grew up eating a lot of kale in soup, so it's sort of amusing how it has become such a trendy veggie in the past 10 years. It's delicious in Kale Soup with Sausage (page 80).

LEMONS: Lemons don't come immediately to mind when thinking about German foods, but it turns out lemon zest and lemon juice are used quite often to add a fresh contrast to creamy sauces. Keep a few around. (It really helps if your generous neighbor has a lemon tree.)

ONIONS: Sometimes it seems as though every German recipe uses onions as a flavor base for roasted meats and gravies.

POTATOES: Germany loves potatoes. When I was growing up in a German household, potatoes were on the table five or six days a week. Imagine that shrimp scene from *Forrest Gump*? Now substitute potatoes . . . boiled potatoes, fried potatoes, potato pancakes, mashed potatoes, potato dumplings. Potatoes even show up in bread!

SUPPENGRÜN: The trinity of leek, carrot, and celeriac (celery root) that finds its way into many soups and stews.

Meat and Dairy

CUTS OF MEAT: Searching for the right cut of meat can be tricky, and it's not just the vocabulary. When you lay an American butcher's carving chart over one from Germany, you notice that things don't always line up. Think about delicious pork roasts with crackling skin: In Germany the *Hals* or *Nacken* (neck) piece is used, but the closest equivalent in America would be the Boston butt (the top of the shoulder). And for pork schnitzel? In Germany, the cut comes from the "ham" part of the pig, but because Americans tend to smoke the ham, a boneless pork cutlet makes a great, and slightly less fatty, substitute.

As for everyone's favorite meal, Braised Beef Rolls (page 90), it's almost impossible to find the perfect precut slices of beef in your grocery store. Ask the butcher to cut a top round roast or London broil horizontally into ¼-inch-thick slabs.

SAUSAGES: For authentic German sausages, unless you have a German sausage maker in your area, or you are confident about sausage making, you might have to use online sources. Fortunately, I am seeing a better selection of sausages in grocery stores that will taste great in German recipes. You can find frankfurters with "snappy" casings, smoked sausage for stews, juicy bockwurst, and an astonishing variety of bratwurst perfect for grilling.

BUTTER AND CREAM: I know we are all watching our calories these days, but butter and cream appear in many of these recipes.

Dry Goods

ALL-PURPOSE FLOUR AND GRANULATED SUGAR: Basic flour and sugar are all you need for these recipes.

BREAD CRUMBS: A surprising number of German recipes call for bread crumbs. Schnitzel and breaded fish are coated in them, and crumbs get added to German Beef Patties (page 84) and the filling of Cabbage Rolls (page 88) to stretch the meat and add moisture. Even Poor Knight (page 26), the German version of French toast, gets a coating of crumbs. You can buy regular unseasoned bread crumbs (panko crumbs are fine), or you can do what my family does and save money by grinding or processing stale bread. Keep your bread crumbs in a sealed container!

CORNSTARCH: It acts as a thickening agent for sauces.

DRY YEAST: In Germany, baking is done with fresh yeast, but these recipes work with the common dry yeast found in American supermarkets.

POWDERED SUGAR: It's great for a simple glaze and often gets sprinkled on finished cakes.

Canned and Jarred Items

ANCHOVY PASTE: This is an essential ingredient for Prussian Meatballs in White Caper Sauce (page 86). A little goes a long way! Fortunately, if you remember to screw the lid back on the tube, it will stay fresh for a long time.

CAPERS: An oddball ingredient you might want to grab are capers. Just a little jar. They go into a few dishes, like Prussian Meatballs in White Caper Sauce (page 86), and I absolutely love them on smoked salmon.

GERMAN PICKLES: Pickles turn up a lot on German tables, both as a crunchy side to a meal and in the recipe. You can't make Cold Potato Salad (page 39) or a *Wurstsalat* (sausage salad) without them, and they are essential in Braised Beef Rolls (page 90). Try to find Hengstenberg Barrel Pickles if you can, but others will do as well.

MUSTARD: Germans put mustard on more than just bratwurst. It goes in all sorts of recipes, from potato salad to sauces. German mustard is best, though a brown mustard or Dijon will do.

SAUERKRAUT: There is no need to make sauerkraut from scratch. There, I said it. But the sauerkraut that comes in a jar in the United States tends to be very salty. Luckily, there are a few tricks in the recipes to Germanize it with a little bacon or butter, cloves, and some wine.

TOMATO PASTE: Some recipes use tomato paste. I suggest buying the kind that comes in a tube. You can use what you need and easily save the rest. However, if you buy it in a can, you can still save the leftovers. Spoon out tablespoon-size blobs onto a piece of plastic wrap. Cover with another piece of plastic wrap and freeze the blobs. Tuck them away in a large zip-top plastic bag, and they'll be ready to use as needed. (Don't forget to label the bag! Because, yes, you will forget what's in there.)

FLAVORINGS AND OILS

BOUILLON: Keep bouillon or soup base in your pantry or refrigerator to "beef up" the flavors in soups and pan gravies. You might think that hearty meat dishes are about the beef or pork, but the magic is often in the sauces that accompany the meat. The Better Than Bouillon brand costs a bit more and needs to stay in the refrigerator, but the flavor is worth it.

DRIED SPICES: In your spice rack, keep bay leaves, caraway seeds, cloves, juniper berries, marjoram, nutmeg, paprika, and white pepper. And for some of those herbs that may not be so common where you shop, I will point out simple substitutions, like thyme for *Bohnenkraut* (summer savory).

SALT AND BLACK PEPPER: Honestly, these are kitchen essentials. I use simple table salt for most of my cooking. Pepper is always best when you grind it yourself, but I promise not to tell if you pour some out of the little jar. You will need peppercorns for a few recipes.

VEGETABLE OIL: These days most recipes seem to call for extra-virgin olive oil, but older German recipes mostly use vegetable oil or, better yet, butter! But you can also use olive oil.

WHITE WINE VINEGAR: Vinegar turns up in a lot of German cooking. Soups get a splash, salads require it, and a lot of other dishes get a shot just to add a balance of acid. Some recipes may call for apple cider vinegar.

SOURCING INGREDIENTS

As much as I wish every dish made with ingredients found in U.S. supermarkets were just like my Oma's cooking, some things just don't taste quite the same. Although I will always provide substitution recommendations where possible in this book, for authentic bread, certain sausages, cheese, and specific seasoning mixes, you may need to find a German store, European deli, or order online. Cost Plus World Market is a great place to find some canned products and sweets, especially during the holidays. And there are some great online sources for ordering specific imported products. I use German-Shop24, Yummy Bazaar, Bavaria Sausage, Usinger's, and the Bread Village most frequently. See page 136 for resources, and find an up-to-date list of online sources for German products on my website (GermanGirlinAmerica.com/german-restaurants-bakeries-delis).

Kitchen Equipment

Most traditional German foods can be prepared with a minimum of fancy equipment. Oma managed with four stovetop burners, a few pots and pans, a paring knife, and her trusty wooden spoon. Of course, she had some special items, like a Spätzle maker and a bread slicer, but most foods don't require a trip to the kitchen supply store. Here are the essentials:

COLANDER: You'll need this for draining noodles or making Spätzle. I like a metal one, but it's up to you.

CUTTING BOARDS: I have a few cutting boards in my kitchen drawer. I usually use two while preparing a meal because of cross-contamination worries with raw meat. Nylon boards get run through the dishwasher to ensure they are clean. I also have a big wooden board for carving roasts and a smaller wooden one that does double duty as a bread cutting board and serving board.

KNIVES: More kitchen accidents happen because of cheap dull knives than anything else (and I have old scars to prove it). You don't need a big set, just a few basic knives that can be sharpened and cared for. An 8-inch chef's knife, a decent serrated bread knife, and a paring knife will cover most of your needs.

ROASTING PAN: It's worth investing in a sturdy one with a removable rack. Bavarian Beer Roasted Pork (page 74) and Marinated Roast Beef (page 92) taste best when roasted or braised in the pan, while Roast Chicken (page 48) and Roasted Christmas Goose (page 60) get that nice crispy skin when raised up on the rack.

SAUCEPANS: Germans and their sauces! Saucepans with handles on both sides are easier to carry to the sink for draining. You'll need them to thicken sauces, boil pasta and potatoes, cook vegetables, and more. Each one should have a lid.

SAUTÉ PANS OR SKILLETS: Keep a few on hand in different sizes. You will need them for everything from frying a schnitzel or potatoes to making pancakes. Small ones are great for sautéing mushrooms or onions that get added to soups or sauces. A good nonstick pan is easier to clean but not essential (provided you use enough butter or oil).

SHEET PANS: If you like baking cookies, German Soft Pretzels (page 28), Homemade Granola (page 22), and your own German Fruit Cake (page 30), then you will need two or three sheet pans. Because I generally use parchment paper, nonstick is not much of an issue. Just note that darker pans might get hotter—watch your baked goods to make sure they don't burn.

SPATULA AND TONGS: These are great for flipping pancakes and grabbing hot meats from the pan.

SPIDER STRAINER: Although the name sounds freaky, this is just a strainer on a handle, useful for pulling dumplings or Spätzle out of boiling water without having to dump everything through a big colander. It's not essential, since a slotted spoon will also do the job.

STOCK/SOUP POTS OR DUTCH OVEN: Soups and one-pot meals are a big part of German cuisine, so you will need a good-size soup pot. A Dutch oven is a nice upgrade but not essential. Make sure your pot has sturdy handles and a lid that fits.

VEGETABLE PEELER: My preference is the peeler with a horizontal blade, because you can just pull the peel off. (Bonus! You can also use the peeler to make chocolate shavings for baked goods.)

WOODEN SPOONS: Keep a few wooden spoons in your arsenal: a regular rounded spoon for normal stirring and a flat-bottomed one to stir thicker mixtures. Remember, nonstick pans don't like metal utensils, so wood is a nice way to keep your nonstick pans from getting scratched.

Specialty Tools and Appliances

Two pieces of equipment that get almost daily use in my kitchen are my stand mixer and food processor. Neither is essential for preparing German foods, but honestly, when you are making Red Cabbage (page 43), running the mounds of cabbage through the feed tube of the processor cuts the job by a lot. Also, I tend to be a multitasker, so the stand mixer can take care of creaming butter while I work on other things.

If you love German Egg Noodles (page 35), you'll find it quicker and easier to make them at home with a Spätzle maker. You can get a decent one (the kind that slides back and forth over a plate with holes) for under $20. If you don't have one, no worries—I'll share some tricks on how to make Spätzle without one.

BEER AND WINE

BEER

One of the earliest food purity laws, the *Reinheitsgebot* (German Purity Law) of 1516, limited German beer to three ingredients: water, hops, and malt. (It took a few years for scientists to understand the importance of yeast, which is now the fourth allowable ingredient.) Yet with only four ingredients, German brewers produce an astonishing variety of good beers. Here are a few great beer varieties:

Bockbier: The strongest beer style in Germany, running from 6 to 10 percent ABV, this malty brew is made to be sipped, not guzzled. The formidable Doppelbock can go as high as 14 percent alcohol.

Helles: The name comes from the German word *hell*, meaning "light" or "pale." A bottom-fermented ale, Helles is characterized by a pleasant, lingering maltiness and has a less prominent hop flavor.

Kölsch: This light, hoppy beer with a crisp finish is associated with Cologne. It's considered a hybrid beer because of the brewing technique, top fermented with ale yeast, then lagered.

Oktoberfest: Traditionally, only the six breweries that produce beer within the Munich city limits can produce Oktoberfest beer. This light-colored beer is traditionally brewed in March and allowed to age until the fall festival. Its flavor is slightly sweet with a gentle nuttiness.

Pilsner (or Pilsen): Named for the Bohemian state, Pilsen is known for its slightly earthy, hop-forward flavor and light straw color.

Rauchbier: This smoked beer gets its distinct flavor from malt roasted over a wood fire instead of in a kiln. You can get Schlenkerla's smoked brews from major US suppliers.

Weissbier (also called Weizenbier or Wheat Beer): Made using at least 50 percent wheat, Weissbier is a yeasty brew with a characteristic citrus flavor (and some say a hint of banana).

WINE

German wine production goes back more than 2,000 years to the days of the Romans in Germany. Seven major wine-growing regions, most notably the Rhine and the Moselle Valley, produce mostly white varietals. Although most people don't think of reds when discussing German wines, varietals like Spätburgunder (similar to pinot noir) and bolder, more tannic Dornfelder go well with German meals. And despite the reputation, German wines are not all sugar sweet!

Grauburgunder and Weisburgunder: My personal favorites, these super drinkable wines have a peachy color and a fruity taste. They're perfect with poultry or just to enjoy on the patio. In the United States, the closest match would be a pinot gris.

Müller-Thurgau: This might be where the "too sweet" reputation comes from. In the 1970s, vintners planted acres of these grapes because of their shorter ripening time. The blends were very sweet, and Germany's wine reputation took a hit as a result.

Riesling: With a flavor that's more citrus than sugar, this is the most common grape varietal in Germany, producing wines that run the spectrum from dry through semisweet to sweet.

Silvaner: Unfortunately, this wine is not well-known on this side of the Atlantic. If you see it, buy it. The fruit-forward flavor is delightful.

About the Recipes

Overall, I've tried to make the recipes in this book as easy as possible so that anyone with minimal experience can achieve great results with basic step-by-step instructions.

Labels

Look for the following labels in the recipes, which will help you plan accordingly:

5-INGREDIENT: Recipes that have five ingredients or fewer, not including salt, black pepper, oil, or water.

30-MINUTE: Recipes that come together in 30 minutes or less, including prep time.

NO-COOK: Recipes that require no cooking. Pulling together an amazing *Brotzeit* takes only a little effort, and you'll never have to turn on the oven.

ONE-POT: Recipes made in one pot or pan. Many of them can be brought to the table in that pot (saving washing up!).

VEGETARIAN OR VEGAN: Despite their reputation for being heavy meat eaters, more and more Germans are choosing to eat vegetarian meals, either full-time or a few times a week. I've included some tasty meatless options in the book.

Tips

You'll also find cooking tips I have learned from my mother or stumbled across on my own:

COOKING TIP: Hints for making a dish easier to prep, cook, or clean up after.

INGREDIENT TIP: Suggestions for substitutions if you can't find the exact ingredients called for in a recipe.

LEFTOVERS TIP: Advice on what to do with any leftover food, especially for recipes that make large portions.

VARIATION TIP: Ideas for changing the flavor of a recipe.

German Fruit Cake *Stollen*, p. 30

CHAPTER 2

BREAKFAST AND BREAD

SOFT-BOILED EGG
Gekochtes Ei

Makes 1 egg | **Prep time:** 5 minutes | **Cook time:** 6 minutes

5-INGREDIENT · 30-MINUTE · ONE-POT · VEGETARIAN

A full German breakfast table will always include soft-boiled eggs served in cute little egg cups. Cut off the top, sprinkle on a little salt, and spoon up the rich creamy yolk along with the smooth egg white. No muss, no sauté pan or skillet—just a few minutes of boiling. Don't have an egg cup? Use a shot glass!

1 egg

1. Fill a small saucepan with enough water to cover the egg completely. Place the pan on the stove over high heat.

2. With a needle, carefully poke a small hole in the fat bottom end of the egg. Place the egg into the saucepan and bring it to a boil. Turn the heat to low and simmer for 3 to 4 minutes for a very soft egg with a runny yolk or 5 to 6 minutes for a barely soft egg with a yolk that's not runny.

3. Drain the boiling water, and run cold water into the pan to stop the cooking.

4. Place the egg in an egg cup and serve.

COOKING TIP: You can keep the cooked egg warm for a while by wrapping it in a kitchen towel. It's best to undercook the egg a little bit if you intend to do so, since it will continue to cook while wrapped.

FARMER'S BREAKFAST
Bauernfrühstück

Serves 4 | **Prep time:** 50 minutes | **Cook time:** 20 minutes

Farmwives created Bauernfrühstück to fill up hungry workers with leftover boiled potatoes mixed with bits of ham and eggs. Feel free to skip the meat and add bell pepper for a hearty vegetarian meal, or add a side salad for a great balanced dinner.

---

3 bacon slices, diced

3 tablespoons butter

1½ pounds russet potatoes, boiled and cut into ⅓-inch-thick slices

1 medium yellow onion, diced

4 ounces ham, diced

6 eggs

3 tablespoons milk

1 tablespoon dried marjoram

4 tablespoons chopped fresh chives, divided

½ teaspoon salt

½ teaspoon freshly ground black pepper

1. In a large sauté pan or skillet over medium heat, cook the bacon for 4 to 5 minutes, or until brown. Add the butter and potatoes and cook for 3 to 4 minutes, turning with a wooden spoon to brown all sides. Add the onion and cook, stirring, until the onion starts to soften. Add the ham and cook for 2 to 3 minutes, stirring, until heated through.

2. While the potato mixture is cooking, in a bowl, whisk together the eggs, milk, marjoram, 2 tablespoons of chives, salt, and pepper.

3. Pour the egg mixture over the potato mixture, stir until evenly coated, and cook for 3 to 4 minutes until the egg is set.

4. Sprinkle with the remaining 2 tablespoons of chives before serving.

HOMEMADE GRANOLA
Müsli

Makes 5 cups | **Prep time:** 10 minutes | **Cook time:** 25 minutes,
plus 30 minutes to cool

VEGETARIAN

Müsli with yogurt and fruit turns up on breakfast buffets all over Germany. The fun part about this recipe is that you can adjust the ingredients to your own tastes. Tangy cherries and crunchy hazelnuts are commonly used in Germany, but you can substitute dried cranberries and almonds. Serve with your favorite low-fat yogurt and some fresh berries, and store any leftovers in an airtight container for up to three weeks.

---

3 cups old-fashioned oats

1 cup sliced almonds

⅓ cup hazelnuts, chopped

⅓ cup unsalted
   sunflower seeds

2 teaspoons ground
   cinnamon

½ cup honey

¼ cup vegetable oil

½ to ¾ cup dried cherries

1. Preheat the oven to 350°F. Line a baking sheet with parchment paper.

2. In a large bowl, mix together the oats, almonds, hazelnuts, sunflower seeds, cinnamon, honey, and oil until evenly coated.

3. Spread the mixture onto the prepared baking sheet and bake for 25 minutes, giving the mixture a stir every 5 minutes or so to ensure that it all gets evenly baked and the nuts don't burn.

4. Sprinkle on the dried cherries, stir until combined, and let cool on the baking sheet for 30 minutes before using.

EGG CAKES OR GERMAN PANCAKES
Eierkuchen

Makes 6 to 8 pancakes | **Prep time:** 5 minutes | **Cook time:** 30 to 40 minutes

5-INGREDIENT · VEGETARIAN

I grew up eating German pancakes, and this recipe is what I believe the morning treat is supposed to look and taste like. Slightly thicker than a crepe, a little crisp at the edges, the pancakes can be filled or topped with nearly anything you can imagine. I love jam, Nutella, a sprinkle of sugar, fruit, or even a savory topping like creamy chicken fricassee. There are entire restaurants in Germany devoted to Eierkuchen and their many toppings. If you're making a savory pancake, simply omit the sugar.

1¾ cups all-purpose flour

4 eggs

2 cups milk

1 tablespoon sugar

3 tablespoons butter or
vegetable oil, divided

1. In a blender, combine the flour, eggs, milk, and sugar and blend until smooth. Let rest for 5 minutes.

2. Melt 1 tablespoon of butter in a medium sauté pan or skillet over medium heat. Pour about ½ cup of batter into the pan and swirl it around to cover the bottom of the pan. The batter should be about ¼ inch thick.

3. Cook until bubbles start to form. Look under an edge of the pancake. If it's golden brown, flip the pancake with a spatula. Cook until the second side is golden brown, another minute or so. Remove and keep warm.

4. Add 1 tablespoon of butter to the pan and repeat the process until all the batter is used.

5. Serve with your topping of choice.

COOKING TIP: If you don't want to make all of the pancakes at one time, you can store uncooked batter for 1 day in the refrigerator. Cover the bowl or blender bowl of batter with plastic wrap or a tight lid. Whisk the batter before using.

APPLE PANCAKES
Apfelpfannekuchen

Makes 7 or 8 pancakes | **Prep time:** 20 minutes | **Cook time:** 45 minutes

VEGETARIAN

To make Apfelpfannekuchen, delicious slices of apple are cooked right into the batter, and the hot pancakes are sprinkled with cinnamon sugar. Add a dollop of whipped cream for an even more special breakfast treat.

2 or 3 crisp apples, peeled, cored, and cut into ¼-inch slices

1 tablespoon freshly squeezed lemon juice

1¾ cups all-purpose flour

4 eggs

2 cups milk

2 tablespoons sugar

Butter, for frying

Cinnamon sugar, for sprinkling

1. Place the apples in a large bowl, sprinkle with the lemon juice, and set aside.

2. In a blender, combine the flour, eggs, milk, and sugar and blend until smooth. Set aside for 5 minutes.

3. Melt 1 tablespoon of butter in a medium sauté pan or skillet over medium heat. Scatter the apples onto the butter, fitting as many in as possible without overlapping. Cook for 1 to 2 minutes, flipping them over halfway through the cooking time.

4. Pour ½ cup of batter over the apples, making sure they're all covered. Cook for 1 to 2 minutes until golden brown on the bottom. Using a spatula, flip the pancake over and cook for about 2 minutes until the second side is golden brown. Transfer to a plate and set aside.

5. Add 1 tablespoon of butter to the pan and repeat the process until all the batter is used. Sprinkle with cinnamon sugar and serve.

COOKING TIP: If you are struggling to flip the pancakes with a spatula, slide the half-cooked pancake onto a dinner plate. Invert the sauté pan over the plate with your other hand, then invert the plate and sauté pan together so the pancake drops into the pan.

THE KAISER'S TORN PANCAKES
Kaiserschmarrn

Serves 4 | **Prep time:** 30 minutes | **Cook time:** 10 minutes

VEGETARIAN

According to legend, these "torn" pancakes get their name from Austrian Kaiser Franz Joseph, who fell in love with them after trying them on a farm. And why not? They are delicious.

½ cup raisins

⅓ cup apple juice, water, or rum

4 eggs, separated

1½ cups all-purpose flour

1 cup milk

Pinch salt

2 teaspoons freshly squeezed lemon juice

2 tablespoons vegetable oil

⅓ to ½ cup powdered sugar

Jam or fruit compote, for serving

1. In a small bowl, combine the raisins and apple juice and set aside.

2. Using a stand mixer fitted with the whisk attachment or a hand mixer, whip the egg whites to stiff peaks. Set aside.

3. Place the flour in a large bowl and make a depression in the center. Put the egg yolks into the depression and whisk until combined. Add the milk, a little at a time, whisking after each addition. Add the salt and lemon juice and whisk until smooth.

4. Using a spatula, fold the egg whites into the yolk mixture in batches.

5. Drain the raisins, add them to the bowl, and fold them into the mixture.

6. Heat the oil in a large sauté pan or skillet over medium heat until it shimmers. Pour the batter into the pan. Cook for 3 to 4 minutes until the pancake browns a bit on the bottom.

7. Using a pan-safe utensil, cut the pancake into fourths and flip the pieces over. Cook for 30 seconds. Move the pieces around, cutting them into smaller pieces and flipping as you do so, until they're cooked through.

8. Sprinkle with powdered sugar and serve with jam or fruit compote.

POOR KNIGHT
(GERMAN FRENCH TOAST)
Arme Ritter

Makes 8 slices | **Prep time:** 5 minutes | **Cook time:** 20 minutes

30-MINUTE · VEGETARIAN

The name of this German version of French toast refers to the poor knights who had to make the best of day-old bread. It's a crunchy, coated breakfast treat that comes to the plate topped with cinnamon sugar and a side of sautéed apples, berries, or jam. (My guy will pour maple syrup on his.)

---

2 eggs, separated

1 cup milk

1 cup sugar, plus
   1 teaspoon

Grated zest of 1 lemon

1 tablespoon water

½ to ¾ cup bread crumbs

1 teaspoon ground
   cinnamon

2 to 4 tablespoons butter or
   vegetable oil

8 (1-inch) slices
   French bread

1. Preheat the oven to 180°F.

2. In a medium bowl, using a fork, whisk together the egg yolks, milk, 1 teaspoon of sugar, and lemon zest. In another medium bowl, whisk together the egg whites and water. Put the bread crumbs in a third medium bowl.

3. In a small bowl, mix together the cinnamon and remaining 1 cup of sugar. Set aside.

4. Melt 2 tablespoons of butter in a large sauté pan or skillet over medium-high heat.

5. Dip both sides of a slice of bread into the egg yolk mixture, then the egg white mixture, then the bread crumbs. Place the coated bread into the sauté pan and repeat until the pan is full.

6. Cook for 1 to 2 minutes until the bread is golden brown. Using a spatula, flip the bread, then cook the other side for 2 to 3 minutes until golden brown. If the bread starts to brown too quickly, lower the heat.

7. Transfer the bread to a serving platter and sprinkle with cinnamon sugar. Place in the oven until ready to serve.

8. Repeat with any remaining bread slices.

GERMAN SOFT PRETZELS
Brezel

Makes 8 pretzels | **Prep time:** 1 hour, plus 1½ hours for the dough to rise
Cook time: 25 minutes

5-INGREDIENT · VEGETARIAN

Pretzels—what could be more German? These have a delightfully chewy crust with a tender inside, perfect for munching on their own or smeared with creamy German Beer Cheese Spread (page 34)! This recipe takes a little time, mostly because of the dough rising, and there is a boiling step in the middle, but it is not complicated, I promise. The result is better than those frozen things at the grocery store, and—bonus!—you can get creative with toppings.

11¼ cups water, divided

2¼ teaspoons dried yeast

2 teaspoons brown sugar

2 tablespoons bread flour, plus 3 cups, plus more for rolling

2 teaspoons salt

Vegetable oil, for oiling the bowl

¼ cup baking soda

¼ cup coarse pretzel salt

1. In a small microwave-safe bowl, warm 1¼ cups of water to about 105°F. Add the yeast, brown sugar, and 2 tablespoons of bread flour and stir until combined. Set aside for 10 minutes.

2. In the bowl of a stand mixer fitted with the paddle attachment, combine the remaining 3 cups of bread flour, salt, and the yeast mixture and mix on low speed until the dough is combined and comes together in a mass.

3. Switch to the dough hook and knead the dough (or knead it by hand) for 10 minutes. Shape the dough into a ball.

4. Coat a medium bowl with oil. Roll the dough in the bowl, making sure to coat the whole ball. Cover the bowl with plastic wrap and place in a warm spot to rise until doubled in size, about 1 hour.

5. While the dough is rising, line 2 baking sheets with parchment paper. Dust a clean work space with a bit of bread flour.

6. Remove the dough from the bowl and cut it into 8 pieces. Take 1 piece of dough and roll and stretch it on the work surface until it's a longish strand. Set it aside to rest a bit and repeat with the remaining dough pieces. Return to the first strand of dough and stretch it a little more until it's 16 to 19 inches long. Repeat with the remaining dough strands.

7. Twist the dough into a pretzel knot by laying a strand in front of you. Arrange the ends in a U shape. Cross one end over the other at the center, so you have an X, but with a round bottom. Fold the ends down and press them into the U bottom a few inches apart so the shape resembles a classic pretzel. Set the pretzel on the prepared baking sheet. Repeat with the remaining dough strands. Set aside and let rise until doubled in size, about 30 minutes.

8. While the pretzels are rising, bring the remaining 10 cups of water to a boil in a non-aluminum pot over high heat. Add the baking soda and stir carefully until it dissolves. Lower the heat to medium so the water simmers.

9. Preheat the oven to 400°F. Position the racks in the oven so there is room for one baking sheet on each level.

10. Using a slotted spoon, lower 2 pretzels into the water, then boil for 30 seconds. Flip over the pretzel and boil for 30 seconds more. Transfer the pretzels to the baking sheet, with the more visually pleasing side faceup.

11. Repeat with the remaining pretzels. Let them rest for 5 minutes.

12. Sprinkle the coarse salt on the pretzels and bake for 10 minutes. Rotate the trays top to bottom and bake for 10 more minutes. Let cool 2 to 3 minutes on the baking sheet. Transfer the pretzels onto cooling racks.

VARIATION TIP: Once you feel comfortable baking pretzels, experiment with toppings. Before baking, instead of salt, sprinkle on shredded Swiss or Parmesan cheese. Place diced ham on the cheese before baking, if you like. Or try a sweet pretzel by sprinkling it with cinnamon sugar.

GERMAN FRUIT CAKE
Stollen

Serves 8 to 10 | **Prep time:** 15 minutes, plus 1 hour 15 minutes for the dough to rest and rise | **Cook time:** 45 minutes

VEGETARIAN

Stollen falls into the mystery space between cake and bread. In Germany, it's synonymous with Christmas, but it's worth making for any festive event.

¾ cup plus
  2 tablespoons milk
4½ cups all-purpose
  flour, divided, plus more
  for rolling
2¼ teaspoons dry yeast
1 teaspoon vanilla extract

1 cup raisins
½ cup chopped candied
  orange peel
½ cup chopped almonds
2 ounces rum or freshly
  squeezed orange juice
¼ cup granulated sugar

1 egg
Grated zest of 1 lemon
½ teaspoon salt
17 tablespoons (2 sticks plus
  1 tablespoon) butter, at
  room temperature, divided
½ cup powdered sugar

1. In a saucepan or microwave-safe dish, heat the milk to 105°F, about a minute on the stovetop or about 30 to 40 seconds in the microwave. Put 3½ cups of flour into the bowl of a stand mixer fitted with the paddle attachment. Make a little well in the flour and put the yeast, vanilla, and milk into it. Sprinkle ¼ cup of flour over the liquid and let it sit for 20 minutes.

2. While waiting, in a medium bowl, mix together the raisins, orange peel, almonds, and rum. Set aside, stirring occasionally.

3. In a small bowl, mix together the granulated sugar, egg, lemon zest, and salt. Pour the sugar mixture over the flour mixture and beat on medium speed until combined. Transfer the mixture to another bowl and let it sit for 15 minutes.

4. Put 15 tablespoons (1 stick plus 7 tablespoons) of butter into the mixer with the remaining ¾ cup of flour and beat them together on low-medium speed until they become a sticky mass. With the mixer on low speed, break off a little of the yeast dough and feed it into the butter dough. Continue to add the yeast dough until it is all fed into the mixer and is combined. Cover with a clean kitchen towel and let rest for 15 minutes.

5. Drain the liquid from the raisin mixture. Add the fruit to the dough and mix until combined. Cover with the kitchen towel and let rest for 15 minutes. Line a baking sheet with parchment paper.

6. Dust a clean work surface with flour and, using a rolling pin, carefully roll the dough into a 12-by-8-inch rectangle. Fold one long side over most of the way, leaving about 2 inches uncovered.

7. Transfer the dough to the prepared baking sheet, seam-side up, cover with a kitchen towel, and let rise until doubled in size, about 30 minutes.

8. Place an oven rack in the second-lowest position. Preheat the oven to 350°F.

9. Bake for 45 minutes, checking at around 40 minutes to make sure the cake's not getting too brown, or until a toothpick inserted into the center comes out clean.

10. Let cool on a cooking rack set on the baking sheet for 5 minutes.

11. Melt the remaining 2 tablespoons of butter and brush it all over the stollen. Sprinkle with the powdered sugar and serve.

Potato Pancakes *Kartoffelpuffer*, p. 38

CHAPTER 3

APPETIZERS AND SIDES

GERMAN BEER CHEESE SPREAD
Obatzda

Serves 4 | Prep time: 10 minutes

NO-COOK · VEGETARIAN

Obatzda, a German cheese spread common in Bavarian beer gardens, is incredibly easy to make. This flavorful spread gets its color from paprika and its pungent flavor from ripe Camembert. Serve it with German Soft Pretzels (page 28) or bread. Plus, it creates a nice base in your stomach for beer.

8 ounces Camembert cheese, at room temperature

6 ounces cream cheese, at room temperature

3 tablespoons butter

¼ cup beer

1 teaspoon paprika

½ teaspoon salt

½ teaspoon freshly ground black pepper

1 teaspoon caraway seeds

Chopped fresh chives, for serving (optional)

Red onion, cut into rings or diced, for serving (optional)

1. Cut the Camembert, cream cheese, and butter into ½-inch pieces, place them in a medium bowl, and mash them together with a fork.

2. Add the beer, paprika, salt, pepper, and caraway seeds and mix until combined.

3. Transfer the mixture to a serving bowl, or scoop it onto a platter. Sprinkle with the chopped chives (if using) and red onion (if using).

4. Store any leftover cheese spread in a sealed container in the refrigerator for up to 4 days.

VARIATION TIP: For a mellower flavor, use Brie instead of Camembert and follow the recipe as instructed.

GERMAN EGG NOODLES
Spätzle

Makes 4 cups | **Prep time:** 15 minutes | **Cook time:** 25 minutes

VEGETARIAN

Spätzle or "little sparrows" are egg noodles that are served alongside many meat dishes to soak up delicious sauces, but they can also be served as a stand-alone dish with a mushroom sauce. The trickiest part of making Spätzle is the shaping. I use an inexpensive Spätzle maker, but you can also scrape the dough through the holes of a colander (see the Cooking Tip) or use a potato ricer.

FOR THE SPÄTZLE

½ teaspoon salt, plus more for the cooking water

1 cup all-purpose flour

6 tablespoons milk

2 eggs

¼ teaspoon ground nutmeg

FOR THE MUSHROOM SAUCE (OPTIONAL)

6 tablespoons (¾ stick) butter, divided

1 pound button mushrooms, brushed clean, ends trimmed, and quartered

3 thyme sprigs

½ cup white or red wine

½ teaspoon salt

½ teaspoon freshly ground pepper

1 garlic clove, minced

2 tablespoons chopped fresh parsley, divided

1 teaspoon chopped fresh chives (optional)

½ teaspoon Maggi seasoning (optional)

TO MAKE THE SPÄTZLE

1. Bring a large pot of salted water to a boil over high heat.

2. In a medium bowl, mix together the flour, milk, eggs, salt, and nutmeg until you get a smooth, sticky batter.

3. When the water is boiling, place a Spätzle maker over the pot of water. Drop a large spoonful of batter into the cup of the spätzle maker and run the cup back and forth over the holes. The batter will fall through the holes into the water. Repeat until all the batter is in the water.

CONTINUED >

4. Lower the heat to medium and simmer for 8 minutes. Using a spider strainer, remove the Spätzle from the water, or drain them in a colander.

TO MAKE THE MUSHROOM SAUCE (IF USING)

5. Melt 3 tablespoons of butter in a large sauté pan or skillet over medium-high heat. Add the mushrooms and the thyme sprigs, and let cook for 7 to 8 minutes, stirring occasionally. You want the mushrooms to release their moisture and brown.

6. Add the wine, salt, and pepper and cook for 1 minute. Turn the heat to low. Add the remaining 3 tablespoons of butter, garlic, 1 tablespoon of parsley, chives (if using), and Maggi (if using). Cook for about 3 minutes over low heat, stirring, until the butter melts and the flavors combine.

7. Remove the thyme sprigs. Sprinkle with the remaining 1 tablespoon of parsley and serve with the Spätzle.

COOKING TIP: To use a colander to shape the Spätzle, place it over the boiling water, drop the batter into the colander, and press or rub the batter through the holes with the back of a spoon. Make sure to clean the colander before draining the Spätzle in step 4.

POTATO DUMPLINGS
Kartoffelklöße

Makes 9 or 10 dumplings | **Prep time:** 40 minutes | **Cook time:** 15 minutes

5-INGREDIENT · VEGETARIAN

Many German home cooks today use instant potato dumplings, but making dumplings from scratch is not difficult, and, honestly, the flavor and texture are so much better. Serve these with any roasted meats, such as Marinated Roast Beef (page 92) or Roasted Christmas Goose (page 60), to soak up the gravy.

---

1 teaspoon salt, plus more
  for the cooking water

2 pounds Yukon Gold
  potatoes, boiled
  and peeled

¾ cup cornstarch or
  potato starch

2 tablespoons butter, at
  room temperature

2 egg yolks

½ teaspoon ground nutmeg

1. Bring a large pot of salted water to a boil over high heat.

2. While the water is boiling, place the potatoes in a large bowl and crush using a ricer or masher.

3. Add the cornstarch, butter, egg yolks, nutmeg, and salt and stir until combined.

4. Wet your hands and knead the potato mixture into a smooth dough.

5. With your hands still wet, break off some of the potato dough and roll it into a 2½- to 3-inch ball. Place it on a plate and repeat until all the dough is used.

6. Lower the heat under the water to medium. You want to maintain a simmer. Using a spider strainer or slotted spoon, lower the dumplings into the water and simmer for 12 to 15 minutes until they float to the top. Remove the dumplings from the water and serve.

LEFTOVERS TIP: To reheat leftovers, cut the dumplings into slices and fry them in butter or bacon fat, as you would fried potatoes. Season generously with salt and pepper for flavor.

POTATO PANCAKES
Kartoffelpuffer

Makes 7 or 8 pancakes | **Prep time:** 20 minutes | **Cook time:** 20 minutes

5-INGREDIENT · VEGETARIAN

Seasoned with onion, these potato pancakes are crispy on the outside, soft and creamy on the inside. Serve as a side dish or as a meal.

1 pound russet
  potatoes, peeled
½ medium yellow
  onion, peeled

2 tablespoons
  all-purpose flour
2 egg yolks
½ teaspoon salt

½ teaspoon freshly ground
  black pepper
Oil, for frying
Chives, for garnish
  (optional)

1. Using a box grater or food processor, grate the potatoes and put them into a medium bowl. Grate the onion into the bowl. Mix the potatoes and onion and drain any liquid. Sprinkle the flour over the potato mixture, add the egg yolks, salt, and pepper and mix.

2. Lay some paper towels on a plate next to the stovetop.

3. Heat ⅓ to ½ inch of oil in a large sauté pan or skillet over high heat until it shimmers.

4. Using a slotted spoon, scoop the potato mixture into the oil, fitting in as many scoops as you can without overcrowding. Using a metal spatula, flatten each scoop into a 4-inch disk. Fry for about 2 minutes until golden brown. Flip over the pancakes and cook for 2 minutes or so until golden brown.

5. Use the slotted spoon to remove the pancakes from the pan and place them on the paper towels to soak up any extra oil. Repeat with the remaining potato mixture.

6. Top with chives, if using, and serve with sour cream or applesauce.

COLD POTATO SALAD
Kartoffelsalat

Serves 4 to 6 | **Prep time:** 45 minutes | **Cook time:** 15 minutes

VEGETARIAN

There are as many recipes for potato salad in Germany as there are German grandmothers. This mayonnaise-based version is typically enjoyed in North and East Germany. My mother serves it alongside a simple sausage or at grill parties.

3 or 4 eggs

1½ pounds russet potatoes, boiled, peeled, and diced

1 medium yellow onion, finely diced

2 to 3 medium German or dill pickles, diced

1 small tart apple, peeled and diced

5 to 7 tablespoons mayonnaise

2 to 3 tablespoons milk

1 tablespoon yellow or German mustard

Salt

Freshly ground black pepper

2 to 4 tablespoons chopped fresh parsley

1. Use a needle to poke a hole into the bottom of the eggs. Fill a saucepan with enough water to cover the eggs completely. Lower the eggs into the water and bring to a boil over high heat. Turn the heat to medium-low and let simmer for 12 minutes. Remove from the heat, replace the hot water with cold water, and let the eggs cool in it for few minutes.

2. Place the potato pieces in a large bowl. Peel the eggs, chop them, and add them to the potatoes. Add the onion, pickles, apple, 5 tablespoons of mayonnaise, 2 tablespoons of milk, mustard, and salt and pepper to taste and mix until the potatoes are coated. Add more mayonnaise or milk as needed.

3. Sprinkle with the parsley and store in the refrigerator until ready to serve.

WARM BAVARIAN POTATO SALAD
Bayerischer Kartoffelsalat

Makes 4 to 5 cups | **Prep time:** 45 minutes | **Cook time:** 15 minutes

This recipe proves that Germans have a very loose interpretation of the word "salad." Still, this side dish is what many people expect from German potato salad. It features slices of potato in a sweet and tangy vinegar sauce studded with bacon. Serve it alongside a grilled bratwurst to turn a simple snack into a meal.

5 ounces bacon (about 5 slices), chopped

1 medium yellow onion, diced

½ cup beef stock

6 tablespoons white wine vinegar

5 tablespoons vegetable oil

1 tablespoon yellow or German mustard

½ teaspoon sugar

1 teaspoon salt

1 teaspoon freshly ground black pepper

2 pounds Yukon Gold potatoes, boiled, peeled, and cut into ⅓-inch-thick slices

2 teaspoons chopped fresh parsley or chives

1. In a sauté pan or skillet over medium heat, cook the bacon for about 3 minutes until it starts to brown. Add the onion and cook, stirring often, until the onion softens and turns translucent. Add the stock, vinegar, oil, mustard, sugar, salt, and pepper and cook for 3 to 4 minutes until heated through.

2. Put the potatoes in a large bowl. Pour the dressing over the potatoes and mix gently until the potatoes are completely coated. Separate any slices that stick together. Sprinkle the parsley over the top and serve warm.

INGREDIENT TIP: Yellow American mustard will work well for this recipe. You can try a "whole seed" mustard for a change of texture and flavor. German mustard will also change the flavor a bit, especially the spicy mustard with horseradish. Experiment and have fun with it!

MEAT SALAD
Fleischsalat

Serves 4 | **Prep time:** 10 minutes

5-INGREDIENT · 30-MINUTE · NO-COOK · ONE-POT

Meat salad? Sure! Traditionally this rich bread topping would be made with left-over beef roast, but these days it's more common to make it with a German bologna-type sausage. This deli staple appears on the table for Abendbrot, the evening meal of bread and cold cuts, or Brotzeit, a midmorning or mid-afternoon hearty snack of bread, pretzels, and cold cuts on bread. Think of it like a tuna or chicken salad but made with sausage. I like serving Fleischsalat like bruschetta as an appetizer on summer afternoons when we are enjoying a beer on the patio.

---

8 to 10 ounces German ring bologna or mortadella

3 or 4 whole German pickles

½ to ¾ cup mayonnaise

2 tablespoons pickle juice, from the jar

½ teaspoon sugar

½ teaspoon salt

½ teaspoon freshly ground black pepper

1. Cut the bologna into thin strips and place them into a medium bowl.

2. Cut the pickles into thin strips and add them to the bowl.

3. Add the mayonnaise, pickle juice, sugar, salt, and pepper and mix until combined.

4. Serve immediately or cover the bowl and let it sit in the refrigerator to develop more flavor.

VARIATION TIP: Mix in ½ yellow onion, diced. Be sure to let it sit in the refrigerator to mellow the flavor before serving.

GREEN BEANS WITH BACON
Speckbohnen

Makes 4 to 5 cups | **Prep time:** 15 minutes | **Cook time:** 15 minutes

5-INGREDIENT · 30-MINUTE

I finally found a way to get kids to eat their green beans—just add bacon! In this recipe, I usually use Speck, which is a smoked pork belly with a prosciutto texture that is common in Germany, but I find that a lean bacon works just as well. I leave my green beans whole (partly because I'm kind of lazy), but you can cut them to 2-inch lengths if you prefer.

Salt

1 pound green beans, ends trimmed

3 ounces (about 3 slices) lean bacon, roughly chopped

1½ cups diced yellow onion

1 summer savory or thyme sprig, or ½ teaspoon dried summer savory or thyme

1 tablespoon butter

½ teaspoon freshly ground black pepper, plus more as needed

1. Bring the beans to a boil in a pot with salted water and cook for 7 to 8 minutes until tender but not mushy. You can also steam them in the microwave.

2. In a large sauté pan or skillet over medium-high heat, cook the bacon until the fat begins to render. Add the onion, stir, and cook for about 2 minutes until the onion is translucent and soft.

3. Drain the beans in a colander and add them to the pan with the bacon and onion. Stir in the summer savory and butter. Add ½ teaspoon salt and the pepper and stir. Let sit for 1 to 2 minutes until the flavors meld.

4. Taste, adjust the seasoning as necessary, and serve.

INGREDIENT TIP: Also known as *Bohnenkraut* (bean herb), summer savory is used in many German dishes containing green beans. Unfortunately, it can be hard to find fresh in the States, but thyme makes a perfectly good substitute.

RED CABBAGE
Rotkohl/Blaukraut

Makes 8 cups | **Prep time:** 15 minutes | **Cook time:** 1 hour

ONE-POT · VEGETARIAN

A classic Christmas recipe, Rotkohl is a cabbage dish with a sweet, lightly tangy flavor that pairs well with meat, especially rich poultry dishes. Making it isn't hard at all. Basically, you throw it all in a pot and let it cook.

1 head red cabbage, cored and cut into ¼-inch shreds

1 medium yellow onion, diced

1 or 2 tart apples, peeled, cored, and diced

2 to 3 tablespoons butter

2 bay leaves

8 to 10 whole cloves

2 tablespoons sugar, plus more as needed

2 to 3 tablespoons apple cider vinegar, plus more as needed

½ teaspoon salt

½ teaspoon peppercorns

½ cup red wine, plus more as needed

1. Pour about 1 inch of water into a large soup pot.

2. Add the cabbage, onion, apples, butter, bay leaves, cloves, sugar, vinegar, salt, peppercorns, and wine to the pot and bring to a boil over high heat.

3. Turn the heat to medium-low, cover, and cook for 30 minutes, stirring occasionally. Taste the cabbage and add more sugar and vinegar to taste.

4. Add more wine, if desired, and cook, stirring occasionally, for another 15 minutes. Taste, and if you like the vegetables a little softer, cook for another 15 minutes.

LEFTOVERS TIP: Store any leftovers in the freezer for up to 3 months. Just thaw and heat to serve.

CUCUMBER SALAD
Gurkensalat

Serves 4 to 6 | **Prep time:** 10 minutes, plus 1 hour to chill

5-INGREDIENT · NO-COOK · ONE-POT · VEGAN

Here is a refreshing and tasty salad that comes together in no time. It's even quicker if you use English cucumbers, because they don't need peeling. Ideally, you should let the flavors meld for a while in the refrigerator but, to be perfectly honest, I sometimes whip this up at the last minute when I realize I need a vegetable dish. It tastes great regardless.

2 cucumbers

¼ cup chopped fresh dill

1 tablespoon dehydrated onion or onion powder, or ¼ cup finely diced onion

2 tablespoons vegetable oil

2 tablespoons white wine vinegar

1 teaspoon salt, plus more as needed

½ teaspoon freshly ground black pepper, plus more as needed

1 teaspoon sugar (optional)

1. If using regular cucumbers, peel them, halve them lengthwise, scrape out the seeds, and cut the cucumbers into ¼-inch slices. If using English cucumbers, cut them into ¼-inch slices. Transfer the cucumber slices to a bowl.

2. Add the dill, onion, oil, vinegar, salt, pepper, and sugar (if using) and stir until the cucumbers are evenly coated.

3. Cover the bowl with plastic wrap and refrigerate for at least 1 hour to mellow the flavors. Stir, taste, and adjust the seasonings, if needed. Serve cold.

CABBAGE SALAD
Krautsalat

Makes 4 to 5 cups | **Prep time:** 10 minutes | **Cook time:** 10 minutes, plus 2 hours to chill

5-INGREDIENT · VEGAN

Krautsalat could be considered the German alternative to coleslaw, with a simple tangy vinaigrette instead of a more creamy dressing. And, as my mother likes to point out, caraway seeds are good for the stomach. You can make this a day in advance to let the flavors really blend.

Salt

1 small to medium head green cabbage

3 tablespoons vegetable oil

3 tablespoons apple cider vinegar or white wine vinegar

½ teaspoon caraway seeds

½ teaspoon freshly ground black pepper, plus more as needed

1. Bring a large soup pot filled with salted water to a boil over high heat.

2. Discard any damaged leaves on the cabbage. Halve it and then cut out the core. Cut the cabbage into four wedges and then cut each wedge into ½-inch strips.

3. When the water is boiling, add the cabbage, turn the heat to low, and cook, stirring occasionally, for 4 minutes. Drain the cabbage and transfer it to a large bowl.

4. Add the oil, vinegar, caraway seeds, ½ teaspoon salt, and pepper to the bowl and mix until the cabbage is evenly coated. Cover the bowl with plastic wrap and refrigerate until completely cooled.

5. Before serving, taste and adjust the seasoning, if needed.

VARIATION TIP: In a hurry? Instead of cooking the cabbage, you can also massage the sliced cabbage with your hands for 10 minutes. This will help break it down a bit, because Krautsalat is not usually eaten raw. If you use this method, you won't need to refrigerate the salad, and it will be ready to eat in under 30 minutes.

Duck Breast in Red Wine Sauce *Entenbrust in Rotweinsoße*, p. 59

POULTRY AND EGGS

ROAST CHICKEN
Brathähnchen

Serves 5 to 6 | **Prep time:** 10 minutes | **Cook time:** 1 hour 15 minutes

Brathähnchen, roasted chicken, comes to the plate with crispy seasoned skin and moist meat. At Oktoberfest, it's called Brathendl, *and if you order it, you'll have half a bird set in front of you. Note: The spice mix here makes enough for four chickens; store the leftovers in a jar with a tight-fitting lid.*

4 teaspoons kosher salt

1 teaspoon freshly ground black pepper

8 teaspoons sweet paprika

3½ teaspoons curry powder

1½ teaspoons chili powder

1 (3½-pound) roasting chicken, giblets removed

4 tablespoons (½ stick) butter, at room temperature, divided

¾ cup water, plus 1 tablespoon

1 tablespoon cornstarch

1. Preheat the oven to 350°F.

2. In a small bowl, mix together the salt, pepper, paprika, curry powder, and chili powder, then set aside.

3. Rub the chicken skin all over with 2 tablespoons of butter. Rub 3 tablespoons of the spice mix all over the chicken and inside the cavity. Set the chicken on a rack in a roasting pan. Put the remaining 2 tablespoons of butter into the pan.

4. Roast for 1 hour, using a pastry brush to baste the skin with butter and drippings every 15 minutes. Cook until the chicken temperature reaches 165°F. Remove the chicken from the pan, leaving the juices behind, and let rest for 5 minutes before carving or cutting into pieces and serving.

5. Add ¾ cup of water to the juices in the roasting pan and scrape up any browned bits. Pour the mixture into a bowl and let sit for 3 to 4 minutes. Skim off the fat, pour the remaining liquid into a small saucepan, and heat to boiling. In a cup, mix together the cornstarch and the remaining 1 tablespoon of water. Add the mixture to the drippings and cook, whisking constantly, until thickened.

CHICKEN FRICASSEE
Hühnerfrikassee

Serves 6 | **Prep time:** 10 minutes | **Cook time:** 25 minutes

During my childhood, my mother often served chicken fricassee—tender chicken, fresh asparagus, and mushrooms in a rich sauce. If you don't have leftover Roast Chicken (page 48) on hand, you can poach two chicken breasts in some chicken stock. Serve this dish over rice or mashed potatoes.

3 tablespoons
   butter, divided
2 tablespoons
   all-purpose flour
4 cups chicken stock
1 bay leaf
2 or 3 whole cloves
8 ounces mushrooms, sliced

¼ cup white wine
2 tablespoons freshly
   squeezed lemon juice
1 teaspoon sugar
2 egg yolks
¼ cup heavy
   (whipping) cream

3 cups shredded
   cooked chicken
8 ounces asparagus, woody
   ends trimmed, cut into
   1- or 2-inch pieces
Salt
Freshly ground
   black pepper

1. Melt 2 tablespoons of butter in a large saucepan over medium heat. Add the flour and whisk until smooth. Add the stock and bring to a boil, whisking constantly. Turn the heat to medium-low, add the bay leaf and cloves, and simmer for 10 to 15 minutes.

2. Melt the remaining 1 tablespoon of butter in a small sauté pan or skillet over medium heat. Add the mushrooms and cook for 4 to 5 minutes, stirring often. Set aside.

3. Remove the bay leaf and the cloves from the stock and discard.

4. Add the wine, lemon juice, and sugar to the stock and stir until combined. In a small bowl, whisk together the egg yolks and cream. Slowly add the mixture to the stock while whisking constantly. Don't let the sauce boil after the cream and egg yolks are added, or the sauce will break.

5. Add the shredded chicken, asparagus, and mushrooms to the pan and stir until combined. Season with salt and pepper to taste and serve.

CHICKEN CORDON BLEU
Hähnchen Cordon Bleu

Serves 4 to 6 | **Prep time:** 20 minutes | **Cook time:** 20 minutes

The original French Cordon Bleu recipe, made with veal, is served flat, with ham and cheese sandwiched between the layers. The Swiss tweaked the recipe by using chicken, and the Germans happily adopted it. This dish is an absolute hit for anyone who loves fried chicken (like my son). It's easy enough for everyday meals but also special enough for company.

4 boneless, skinless
  chicken breasts
4 slices Black Forest ham
4 slices Gruyère or
  Swiss cheese

Salt
Freshly ground
  black pepper
½ cup all-purpose flour
2 eggs

2 teaspoons cream or milk
1 cup bread crumbs
2 tablespoons vegetable oil

1. Lay a chicken breast on a cutting board. Using a sharp knife, slice into it parallel to the cutting board almost all the way through, so that you can fold it open like a book. Cover with plastic wrap and use a meat hammer or the flat bottom of a saucepan to flatten it. Repeat with the other breasts.

2. Place a slice of ham on each chicken breast and top with a slice of cheese. Fold the chicken over the ham and cheese (like closing a book) and secure with a toothpick. Season with salt and pepper.

3. Put the flour in a small bowl. In a second small bowl, beat the milk and eggs. Put the bread crumbs in a third small bowl. Dip the chicken pieces, one at a time, first in the flour, then in the eggs, then in the bread crumbs. Press the bread crumbs in a little bit to make sure they stick. Place the chicken pieces on a plate.

4. Heat the oil in a large sauté pan or skillet over medium-high heat until it shimmers. Place the chicken pieces into the pan, making sure not to overcrowd them. Cook for 2 to 3 minutes. Turn over the chicken and cook on the other side for 2 to 3 minutes. Turn them over again, lower the heat to medium, and cook for 5 minutes. Turn them over one more time and cook for 5 minutes. Remove the toothpicks and serve immediately.

LEFTOVERS TIP: These reheat well. Store any leftovers in an airtight container in the freezer for up to 1 month. When you are ready, remove the pieces from the freezer and let them thaw in the refrigerator. Reheat them on the stovetop in a little oil over medium heat for 2 minutes per side.

CHICKEN IN RIESLING SAUCE
Hähnchenbrust in Rieslingsoße

Serves 4 to 6 | **Prep time:** 15 minutes | **Cook time:** 25 minutes

30-MINUTE · ONE-POT

This recipe marries the Germans' love for wine, cream, and sauce perfectly. The chicken is just there to give the sauce something to hang on to. It's a meal that appeals to adult palates but also works with kids, since the alcohol in the wine cooks off. Serve over rice.

2 pounds boneless, skinless chicken breasts

2 tablespoons butter

Salt

Ground white pepper or freshly ground black pepper

3 bacon slices, diced

½ cup diced onion

1 cup sliced mushrooms

1 tablespoon all-purpose flour

2 cups Riesling wine

1 thyme sprig, or 1 teaspoon dried thyme

1 teaspoon grated lemon zest

½ cup heavy (whipping) cream

1. Using a sharp knife, halve the chicken breasts parallel to the cutting board, and then halve each slice again. (You want the chicken to be in thin slices, almost like cutlets.) Melt the butter in a large sauté pan or skillet over medium-high heat. Season the chicken with salt and pepper. Add the chicken to the pan and cook for 3 to 4 minutes on each side until it starts to brown. Transfer the chicken to a plate and set aside.

2. Add the bacon and onion to the pan and cook for 4 to 5 minutes, stirring often, until the bacon is browned and the onion is translucent. Add the mushrooms and cook, stirring often, for 3 minutes.

3. Add the flour to the pan and stir until combined. Add the Riesling and stir to loosen up the browned bits in the pan. Add the thyme and lemon zest and cook, stirring constantly, for 3 minutes. Add the cream and stir until combined. Season with salt and pepper to taste. Return the chicken to the pan, lower the heat to medium, and simmer for 2 minutes. Serve hot.

CHICKEN IN CREAMY MUSHROOM SAUCE
Hähnchen Geschnetzeltes

Serves 4 | **Prep time:** 10 minutes | **Cook time:** 15 minutes

30-MINUTE · ONE-POT

Geschnetzeltes is a favorite. One time when I was on a tour of Germany, I was served this creamy chicken dish three nights in a row, and I wasn't at all mad. The recipe arrived in Germany via Switzerland, where they traditionally make it with veal. Serve with German Egg Noodles (page 35).

1 pound chicken cutlets, cut into ¼-inch strips

Salt

Freshly ground black pepper

2 tablespoons vegetable oil

2 tablespoons butter

¼ to ½ medium yellow onion, finely diced

8 ounces sliced mushrooms

1 tablespoon all-purpose flour

1 cup chicken stock

¾ cup heavy (whipping) cream

Chopped fresh parsley, for serving

1. Season the chicken with a little salt and pepper. Heat the oil in a large sauté pan or skillet over medium-high until it shimmers. Add the chicken and cook, stirring often, for 3 to 4 minutes. Transfer the chicken to a plate.

2. Add the butter to the pan to melt. Add the onion and mushrooms and cook for about 4 minutes until soft.

3. Remove the pan from the heat and add the flour. Using a wooden spoon, stir until combined. Stir in the stock until combined. Return the pan to medium-high heat, add the cream, and stir until combined. Turn the heat to medium-low and return the chicken plus any juices from the plate to the pan. Simmer for 5 minutes. Taste and add more salt and pepper, if needed. Sprinkle with the parsley and serve.

VARIATION TIP: Experiment with different proteins, like turkey or pork. The same goes for other varieties of mushrooms: I love this dish with chanterelles or shiitakes.

CHICKEN DÖNER
Hähnchen Döner

Serves 6 | **Prep time:** 15 minutes, plus 8 hours to marinate | **Cook time:** 40 minutes

In some German cities it seems like there is a Döner stand on every other corner. Boldly seasoned and roasted, the shaved meat is served piled high in a pita-like bread along with vegetable toppings and sauces. Döner arrived in Germany via Turkish immigrants, and though making this chicken Döner at home isn't the same as ordering from a train station Imbiß (takeaway booth), it will have to do until your next trip.

FOR THE DÖNER

2½ to 3 pounds boneless, skinless chicken thighs

1 cup plain yogurt or sour cream

1 teaspoon freshly squeezed lemon juice

2 teaspoons paprika

2 teaspoons ground cumin

2 teaspoons ground coriander

2 teaspoons onion powder

1 teaspoon chili powder

2½ tablespoons tomato paste

1½ teaspoons salt

½ teaspoon freshly ground black pepper

2 or 3 garlic cloves, minced

Vegetable oil, for grilling

FOR SERVING

Pita bread or lavash

Diced tomato

Shredded lettuce

Diced cucumber

Tzatziki

Hummus

Hot sauce (optional)

TO MAKE THE DÖNER

1. Rinse and pat dry the chicken thighs. Trim off any excess fat. Place the chicken in a gallon-size zip-top bag.

2. In a medium bowl, mix together the yogurt, lemon juice, paprika, cumin, coriander , onion powder, chili powder, tomato paste, salt, pepper, and garlic. Add the mixture to the bag with the chicken, seal, and knead the bag until the chicken is completely coated. Set the bag on a plate and refrigerate for at least 8 hours.

3. Thirty minutes before you are ready to cook, soak wooden skewers in water so they don't burn on the grill. Preheat a grill. If you are using a gas grill, heat only half of the grill. If you are using charcoal, move the coals to one side.

4. Remove the chicken thighs from the bag. On a cutting board, roll each thigh lengthwise into a semi-tight roll. Secure by pushing 2 skewers through the roll, about 1 inch apart, so the thigh is secured by the skewer. Add 1 or 2 more rolled-up thighs to each set of skewers.

5. When the grill is hot, brush the grill with oil. Place the chicken skewers over indirect heat. Cook for 40 minutes, rotating every 10 to 15 minutes. Remove from the grill when thoroughly cooked.

TO SERVE

6. While the chicken is cooking, preheat the oven to 200°F. Place the pita in the oven to warm.

7. When the chicken is cooked, remove it from the skewers and cut it into slices. Place the warm pita on individual pieces of aluminum foil. Top each with chicken, tomato, lettuce, cucumber, tzatziki, hummus, and hot sauce (if using).

VARIATION TIP: Instead of filling a pita, build a salad with the döner meat and other toppings.

SCHNITZEL WITH HUNTER'S SAUCE
Schnitzel mit Jägersoße

Serves 4 | **Prep time:** 20 minutes | **Cook time:** 50 minutes

Mushroom foraging in Germany is an old tradition, and in autumn the woods can get crowded with folks searching for edible Waldpilze (forest mushrooms). These are often used to make Jägersoße, a rich flavorful sauce, but mushrooms bought at the grocery store or farmers' market will work just as well for this recipe, which elevates simple Schnitzel to a hearty, comforting feast.

1 pound boneless, skinless chicken breast or scallops of turkey breast

¾ cup all-purpose flour

2 eggs, beaten

1 cup bread crumbs

Salt

Freshly ground black pepper

2 tablespoons vegetable oil, divided

5 tablespoons (½ stick plus 1 tablespoon) unsalted butter, divided

1 cup diced onion

1 pound sliced mushrooms

1 cup chicken or vegetable stock

½ cup heavy (whipping) cream

1 tablespoon cornstarch

1 teaspoon water

1. Line a cooling rack with paper towels and set aside. Using a meat hammer or the bottom of a heavy saucepan, pound the poultry to around ⅓ inch thick.

2. Put the flour in a small bowl, the eggs in another bowl, and the bread crumbs in a third bowl. Lightly season the chicken pieces with salt and pepper, then one at a time, dip the poultry pieces into the flour, then the eggs, and finally the bread crumbs. Place each coated chicken piece on a large plate.

3. Heat 1 tablespoon of oil and 1 tablespoon of butter in a large skillet over medium-high heat until the mixture starts to shimmer. Place half of the chicken in the pan, making sure not to overcrowd it. Cook for about 4 minutes until the chicken is browned. Flip over the chicken and cook for 4 to 6 minutes until browned. Transfer the cooked chicken to the prepared cooling rack. Season both sides lightly with salt. Repeat with the remaining 1 tablespoon of oil, 1 tablespoon of butter, and the remaining chicken pieces.

4. Melt the remaining 3 tablespoons of butter in a large saucepan over medium heat. Add the onion and sauté for 5 to 7 minutes. Add the mushrooms and sauté for 3 minutes. Add the stock, stirring to scrape up any browned bits on the bottom. Turn the heat to medium-low and simmer for 10 minutes.

5. Add the cream, stir, and season with salt and pepper to taste. Cook for about 4 minutes, making sure the mixture doesn't boil, until the sauce reduces and thickens. In a cup, mix together the cornstarch and water. Add the mixture to the sauce and cook, stirring constantly, until thickened. Ladle some of the sauce on the chicken and serve the rest on the side.

EGGS IN MUSTARD SAUCE
Eier in Senfsoße

Serves 4 | **Prep time:** 5 minutes | **Cook time:** 20 minutes

30-MINUTE · VEGETARIAN

Flavorful meat-free recipes like this one filled hungry bellies in Germany during times when meat was hard to come by, and traditional Catholic families also served them on "meatless Fridays." Plus, these eggs also happen to make a great brunch dish! Serve them with boiled potatoes or toast for a simple, satisfying meal.

---

8 eggs

2 tablespoons unsalted butter

2 tablespoons all-purpose flour

1 cup vegetable stock

1 cup milk

3 tablespoons German or yellow mustard

Salt

Chopped fresh parsley, for garnish

1. Prick the large end of each egg with a needle or tack. Set the eggs in a large pot, add enough water to just cover them, and bring to a boil over medium-high heat. Lower the heat to medium and simmer for 9 minutes.

2. Pour out the water, and stop the cooking process by covering the eggs with cold water. Drain and set aside.

3. While the eggs are cooking, melt the butter in a saucepan over medium heat. Whisk in the flour until no lumps are present. Keep whisking while you pour in the stock and milk. Cook for about 2 to 3 minutes, until the sauce begins to thicken. Add the mustard and whisk until combined. Taste, and season with salt, if needed.

4. Peel the eggs and cut them in half. Place four egg halves on each plate, spoon over some sauce, sprinkle with fresh parsley, and serve.

DUCK BREAST IN RED WINE SAUCE
Entenbrust in Rotweinsoße

Serves 4 | **Prep time:** 15 minutes | **Cook time:** 40 minutes

ONE-POT

I had this dish at a Michelin-starred restaurant in the Black Forest, and I swear I licked the plate. Serve it with Red Cabbage (page 43) and mashed potatoes.

2 pounds boneless, skin-on duck breast

2 tablespoons butter

Salt

Freshly ground black pepper

2 shallots, diced

3 thyme sprigs, or 2 teaspoons dried thyme

1 teaspoon tomato paste

6 juniper berries

½ cup red wine

1½ cups chicken stock

1 tablespoon cornstarch

1 tablespoon water

1. Rinse and pat dry the duck breasts. Prick the skin with a fork a few times. Melt the butter in a large sauté pan or skillet over medium heat. Add the duck breasts, skin-side down, and cook for 5 minutes.

2. While the breasts are cooking, season them with salt and pepper. Flip them over, add the shallots to the pan, and add more salt and pepper. Cook for 2 minutes, stirring the shallots.

3. Transfer the duck and shallots to a plate. Pour off all but 2 tablespoons of fat and discard. Add the thyme, tomato paste, berries, wine, and stock to the pan and stir, scraping the browned bits from the bottom. Bring to a boil, stirring often. Turn the heat to low and simmer.

4. Return the duck breasts and shallots to the pan, cover, and cook for 15 to 20 minutes until the internal temperature reaches between 135°F and 140°F. Transfer the duck to a plate and cover with aluminum foil.

5. Raise the temperature to medium-high. In a cup, mix together the cornstarch and water. When the stock starts to bubble, add the cornstarch mixture and stir until thickened.

6. Cut the duck into ½-inch slices and serve with the sauce.

ROASTED CHRISTMAS GOOSE
Weihnachtsgans

Serves 4 to 6 | **Prep time:** 25 minutes | **Cook time:** 1 hour 45 minutes

Traditionally, goose gets served twice a year in Germany: on Christmas Day and on November 11, St. Martin's Day. As the story goes, St. Martin didn't want to be a bishop, so he hid in a barn with some geese. The geese gave away his hiding place with their honking, so now we eat goose on his feast day. (I'm sure there is a moral in there somewhere.)

1 (8- to 9-pound) goose
Salt
Freshly ground
 black pepper
2 teaspoons dried thyme

2 onions, one halved, the
 other chopped
1 apple, peeled, cored,
 and chopped

1 cup water, plus
 1 tablespoon
3 cups chicken stock
1 tablespoon cornstarch
 (optional)

1. Preheat the oven to 350°F.

2. Rinse the goose and pat it dry. Remove the giblets and set them aside. Trim off the neck, cut off the tips of the wings, and set them aside. Trim any excess fat from around the opening and the tail, reserving some of it for the gravy. Prick the skin of the goose all over with a fork, and season the whole thing (including the cavity) with salt, pepper, and the thyme. Stuff the cavity with the onion halves and the apple.

3. Pour 1 cup of water into a roasting pan, place a rack in the pan, and place the goose on the rack. Roast for 1¾ hours, basting occasionally with the juices from the pan.

4. While the duck is roasting, make the gravy. In a saucepan, combine the neck and wing tips, some of the trimmed fat, and the gizzards. Add the chopped onion and cook for about 5 minutes over medium-high heat until browned. Add the stock and bring to a boil. Turn the heat to medium-low and let cook, stirring occasionally, for 1 hour. Strain the gravy through a fine-mesh sieve set over a bowl. Discard the solids. If you like a thicker gravy, combine the cornstarch and the remaining 1 tablespoon of water in a cup. Raise the heat to medium-high, and when the gravy starts bubbling, whisk in the cornstarch mixture until the gravy is smooth. Taste and season with salt or pepper, if needed.

5. The goose is done when the temperature reaches between 165°F and 170°F. Let rest for a few minutes before carving into slices.

COOKING TIP: A goose is carved differently than a turkey. Remove the breast meat by cutting it out whole, then cut it into slices. The leg and wings are cut at the joints. The thigh is removed and cut into slices.

Bavarian Beer Roasted Pork *Bayerischer Krustenbraten*, p. 74

CHAPTER 5

PORK

BRATWURST AND SAUERKRAUT
Bratwurst und Sauerkraut

Serves 6 | **Prep time:** 15 minutes | **Cook time:** 1 hour 15 minutes

Bratwurst and sauerkraut just go together. Yes, you can throw the brats on a grill and call it a day, but because they are made from raw meat, it's not a bad idea to precook them a bit to make sure they are done and to keep the skin from splitting. There are lots of options for bratwurst in American grocery stores these days, including flavors like jalapeño or chicken apple. I tend to stick with basic brats, but this technique should work with any of them. The sausages can be served on their own or in rolls.

FOR THE SAUERKRAUT

1 (24-ounce) jar or refrigerated package sauerkraut

3 tablespoons butter, or 3 bacon slices, diced

1 medium yellow onion, diced

3 or 4 bay leaves

5 or 6 juniper berries

4 or 5 whole cloves

½ cup sweet white wine or water

Salt

Freshly ground black pepper

FOR THE BRATWURST

6 bratwurst

1 (12-ounce) bottle lager or weizen beer (optional)

1 tablespoon vegetable oil (if pan-frying)

Mustard, for serving

TO MAKE THE SAUERKRAUT

1. Drain the sauerkraut in a colander or fine-mesh sieve. Rinse it under running water and let it drain again. Press some of the excess moisture out.

2. Melt the butter in a large saucepan over medium heat. If you're using bacon instead, cook the bacon for 4 to 5 minutes over medium heat until brown. Add the onion and cook for 3 to 4 minutes until softened and translucent.

3. Add the drained sauerkraut, bay leaves, juniper berries, cloves, wine, and enough water to just cover the top of the sauerkraut, stir until combined, and bring to a simmer. Cook the sauerkraut, stirring occasionally, for at least 30 minutes and up to 1 hour. You may need to add more water or wine if it evaporates too quickly. Taste and add salt and pepper, if needed.

4. Precooking the bratwurst before frying or grilling them is optional, but to do so, pour the beer and the same amount of water into a large sauce-pan (if not using beer, pour in 3 cups of water). Add the sausages and bring just to a boil over medium-high heat. Immediately turn the heat to medium-low and simmer for 10 minutes. Then fry or grill until the skin is brown and crispy.

5. If you are frying the bratwurst, heat the oil in a sauté pan or skillet over medium heat, add the sausage, and fry for about 8 minutes until well browned all over. If you are grilling the bratwurst, place them on a hot grill and cook, turning often, until cooked through, about 8 minutes.

6. Remove the bay leaves, juniper berries, and whole cloves from the sauerkraut. Serve the bratwurst with the sauerkraut and mustard on the side.

VARIATION TIP: For a sweet sauerkraut, peel, core, and chop an apple and add it to the pan with the onion. The apple will cook down and blend with the cabbage.

BRATWURST WITH CURRY SAUCE
Currywurst

Serves 6 | **Prep time:** 10 minutes | **Cook time:** 20 minutes

30-MINUTE

Since its invention in 1949, Currywurst has been a favorite late-night snack or quick lunch all over Germany. My favorite stand is next to the train station by the KaDeWe in Berlin, but until I can get back there, this satisfies my cravings. Serve over French fries for an authentic Currywurst experience.

1½ cups ketchup

1 tablespoon tomato paste

2 tablespoons curry powder, divided

1 teaspoon onion powder

¼ cup beef stock

1 teaspoon Worcestershire sauce

½ teaspoon chili powder or cayenne pepper (optional)

6 bratwurst or bockwurst

1 tablespoon vegetable oil (if pan-frying)

1. In a medium saucepan over low heat, combine the ketchup, tomato paste, 1½ tablespoons of curry powder, onion powder, stock, and Worcestershire sauce. Raise the heat to medium, stir, and cook until it begins to bubble. Stir in the chili powder if you like it spicy and simmer for 20 minutes.

2. Precooking the bratwurst before frying or grilling them is optional, but to do so, pour 3 cups of water into a large saucepan. Add the sausages and bring just to a boil over medium-high heat. Immediately turn the heat to medium-low and simmer for 10 minutes.

3. If frying the bratwurst, heat the oil in a sauté pan over medium heat, add the sausages, and fry for about 8 minutes until browned and crisp all over. If grilling the bratwurst, place them on a hot grill and cook for about 8 minutes, turning often, until browned and crisp all over.

4. Cut the sausages into bite-size slices. Serve smothered in the curry sauce, and sprinkle the remaining ½ tablespoon of curry powder on top.

FILLED GERMAN DUMPLINGS
Maultaschen

Makes 25 dumplings | **Prep time:** 30 minutes to 1 hour | **Cook time:** 30 to 45 minutes

Some people describe Maultaschen as ravioli, but my daughter calls them German pot stickers. Serve them in a simple beef stock or, after cooking, crisp them in a skillet with melted butter.

3 bacon slices, chopped

½ yellow onion, diced

3 garlic cloves, minced

8 ounces frozen spinach

1 tablespoon dried marjoram

1 teaspoon dried thyme

2 tablespoons chopped fresh parsley

¼ teaspoon ground nutmeg

1 pound ground pork

2 eggs

¼ cup bread crumbs

1 teaspoon salt

1 teaspoon freshly ground black pepper

4 cups beef stock

50 wonton wrappers

Chopped fresh parsley, for serving

1. In a large sauté pan over medium heat, cook the bacon for 2 minutes. Add the onion and cook for 2 to 3 minutes until translucent. Add the garlic, spinach, marjoram, thyme, parsley, and nutmeg and cook, stirring often, until the spinach is wilted. Transfer the mixture to a bowl. Add the ground pork, 1 egg, bread crumbs, salt, and pepper and stir until combined.

2. Pour the stock into a large soup pot over medium heat. In a small bowl, beat the remaining 1 egg.

3. Drop 1 tablespoon of filling into the center of a wonton wrapper. Using a pastry brush, paint the edge with a little beaten egg, then top with another wonton wrapper. Seal the edges with your fingers or a fork. Repeat with the remaining filling and wonton wrappers.

4. Bring the stock to a simmer. Add 5 or 6 dumplings and simmer for 10 minutes. Using a slotted spoon, transfer the dumplings to a plate. Repeat until all the dumplings are cooked. Fill bowls with about ½ cup of stock and 4 or 5 dumplings. Sprinkle with parsley and serve.

PORK MEDALLIONS WITH MUSHROOM CREAM SAUCE
Schweinelendchen mit Pilzrahmsoße

Serves 4 | **Prep time:** 10 minutes | **Cook time:** 25 minutes

30-MINUTE · ONE-POT

I learned how to make Schweinelendchen from my Tante (aunt), and honestly, this creamy pork and mushroom dish is a great recipe to have in your back pocket. It's relatively quick and inexpensive, yet it looks fancy enough for company. The recipe can easily be doubled, and the leftovers taste amazing.

1½ pounds pork tenderloins

Salt

Freshly ground
  black pepper

4 tablespoons (½ stick)
  butter, divided

1 onion, diced

2 cups sliced mushrooms

½ cup white wine

⅔ cup beef or
  vegetable stock

¾ cup heavy
  (whipping) cream

Splash Cognac (optional)

3 tablespoons chopped
  fresh parsley

1. Rinse and pat dry the pork tenderloins and cut them into 1-inch-wide slices or medallions. Lightly season the pork with salt and pepper.

2. Melt 2 tablespoons of butter in a large sauté pan or skillet over medium-high heat. Add the pork medallions and cook for about 3 minutes on each side until browned. Transfer the medallions to a plate and cover to keep warm.

3. Melt the remaining 2 tablespoons of butter in the sauté pan over medium-high heat. Add the onion and cook for about 2 minutes, stirring often, until translucent. Add the mushrooms and cook for 5 minutes, stirring often. Add the wine, stir, making sure to scrape up any browned bits on the bottom, and cook for 2 to 3 minutes until the liquid reduces a bit. Add the stock, heavy cream, and Cognac (if using) and cook, stirring, for 4 minutes. Add the parsley, stir until combined, and serve.

PORK SCHNITZEL WITH BELL PEPPER SAUCE
Paprikaschnitzel

Serves 4 | **Prep time:** 20 minutes | **Cook time:** 25 minutes

ONE-POT

My favorite restaurant in Berlin (Elefant) serves at least 15 different versions of Schnitzel, including Paprikaschnitzel, which isn't breaded but, rather, dusted with paprika and smothered in a sauce of bell peppers and onion.

4 to 6 boneless pork chops

Salt

Freshly ground
   black pepper

1½ tablespoons
   paprika, divided

3 tablespoons vegetable
   oil, divided

1 medium yellow onion,
   thinly sliced

1 red bell pepper,
   thinly sliced

1 green bell pepper,
   thinly sliced

1 garlic clove, chopped

2 tablespoons tomato paste

1 tablespoon
   all-purpose flour

½ cup chicken or beef stock

½ cup heavy
   (whipping) cream

1. Using a meat hammer, pound the pork chops until they are about ⅓ inch thick. Season them with salt, pepper, and ½ tablespoon of paprika.

2. Heat 2 tablespoons of oil in a large sauté pan or skillet over medium-high heat. Cook the pork chops for 3 minutes on each side, transfer them to a plate, and cover with aluminum foil. Heat the remaining 1 tablespoon of oil in the pan over medium-high heat. Add the onion, red bell pepper, and green bell pepper and cook for 5 to 6 minutes, stirring, until the vegetables soften.

3. Stir in the remaining 1 tablespoon of paprika, garlic, tomato paste, flour, and stock and bring to a boil, scraping up any browned bits on the bottom. Turn the heat to medium-low, add the cream, ½ teaspoon of salt, and ½ teaspoon of pepper and stir until combined. Return the pork to the pan and cook for 2 to 3 minutes until heated through. Serve immediately with potatoes or rice.

WESTPHALIAN SCHNITZEL WITH EGG
Westfalisches Krüstchen

Serves 4 | **Prep time:** 15 minutes | **Cook time:** 15 minutes

30-MINUTE

Westfalisches Krüstchen takes a simple flattened, breaded chop, sets it on toasted bread, and tops it with a fried egg. When you cut into the egg, the yolk oozes down and makes a sort of rich "sauce." Serve with fried potatoes and a mixed salad.

4 boneless pork chops

Salt

Freshly ground
   black pepper

¼ cup all-purpose flour

9 eggs

½ cup bread crumbs

4 slices white or
   whole-wheat bread

2 tablespoons butter, plus
   more for spreading

3 tablespoons vegetable oil

1. Rinse and pat dry the pork chops. Using a meat hammer, pound the pork chops to thin them. Season with salt and pepper.

2. Put the flour in a small bowl. In a second small bowl, beat 5 eggs. Put the bread crumbs in a third small bowl. Dip a chop into the flour, covering both sides, and shake off any excess. Then, dip it into the beaten eggs, covering both sides, followed by the bread crumbs, making sure to pat them into the meat. Transfer to a plate. Repeat with the remaining chops.

3. Toast the bread, butter it, and arrange the slices on a serving platter.

4. Heat the oil in a large sauté pan or skillet over medium-high heat until the oil shimmers. Place the breaded chops into the pan and fry for 3 to 4 minutes on each side. Place a chop on each slice of toast.

5. Melt the remaining 2 tablespoons of butter in another skillet over medium heat. Crack the remaining 4 eggs into the skillet. Cook for about 3 minutes until the egg whites are no longer clear. Flip over the eggs and cook for 30 seconds longer. Place an egg on each pork chop and serve.

MARINATED GRILLED PORK STEAKS
Schwenker Marinade

Serves 6 | **Prep time:** 15 minutes, plus 12 to 24 hours to marinate
Cook time: 15 to 30 minutes, depending on the cut

In Germany, grilling is an event, especially when using a Schwenker grill. Think of it as campfire cooking with a twist. The grill surface hangs by a chain over an open fire, while the person in charge of the grill Schwenkt (swings) it to keep things moving. But your regular grill at home will work just as well. The flavorful marinade in this recipe takes me back to summers in Opa's garden.

½ cup vegetable oil

1½ onions, cut into rings

2 garlic cloves, smashed

½ teaspoon dried thyme

½ teaspoon dried oregano

4 bay leaves

4 juniper berries, crushed

1 teaspoon salt

½ teaspoon peppercorns

½ teaspoon paprika

1 shot obstler (optional; see Ingredient Tip)

6 pork steaks or country-style ribs

1. In a medium bowl, mix together the oil, onions, garlic, thyme, oregano, bay leaves, juniper berries, salt, peppercorns, paprika, and obstler (if using). Pour into a gallon-size zip-top plastic bag. Add the meat to the bag, seal, and refrigerate for 12 to 24 hours.

2. Preheat your grill.

3. Remove the meat from the marinade and discard the marinade. Grill the steaks for 6 or 7 minutes per side. Country-style ribs will take longer, maybe 8 to 10 minutes per side.

INGREDIENT TIP: Obstler is a German clear fruit brandy. It's not sweet, but it is quite strong. A shot in the marinade is optional, though a shot in the grill master is almost mandatory in Germany.

VARIATION TIP: This marinade also works well on pork tenderloins, chicken breasts, and even vegetables.

MUSTARD ROASTED PORK LOIN
Senfbraten

Serves 6 | **Prep time:** 10 minutes | **Cook time:** 1 hour 50 minutes

Senfbraten is one of those easy recipes everyone should keep in their back pocket. Serve it with mashed or boiled potatoes or make some Potato Dumplings (page 37).

2 pounds pork loin roast
Salt
Freshly ground
  black pepper
1 teaspoon dried thyme

3 tablespoons
  German mustard
2 tablespoons butter
1 onion, diced
1 or 2 carrots, cut
  into chunks

2 garlic cloves, chopped
1 cup beef stock
1¾ cups water, divided, plus
  1 teaspoon
1 teaspoon cornstarch

1. Preheat the oven to 350°F.

2. Rinse the meat and pat dry with paper towels. Sprinkle all over with salt, pepper, and the thyme and spread the mustard all over the meat.

3. Melt the butter in a metal roasting pan over medium-high heat on the stovetop. Place the pork, fat-side down, in the pan and cook for 2 to 3 minutes until browned. Rotate the roast and continue cooking for 2 to 3 minutes on each side until all sides have been browned. Add the onion carrots, and garlic and cook, stirring constantly, for 3 minutes. Add the stock and ¾ cup of water, cover the pan with aluminum foil, and place in the oven.

4. Roast for 1 hour, checking periodically to add water if it looks dry. Remove the foil. Roast for another 30 minutes until a thermometer reads 160°F. Transfer the roast to a plate or carving board, cover with foil, and let rest.

5. Add 1 cup of water to the pan. Using a wooden spoon, scrape up the browned bits in the pan. Pour everything into a medium saucepan. Cook the sauce over medium-high heat. In a cup, mix the cornstarch in the remaining 1 teaspoon of water, then add the mixture to the sauce while whisking constantly. When the sauce is thick, taste, and add salt and pepper, if needed.

6. Cut the meat into slices. Spoon some sauce over the roast and serve more on the side.

INGREDIENT TIP: I use Bautz'ner mustard from Germany, but any German mustard will do. Don't have any? You can use Dijon or brown mustard.

BAVARIAN BEER ROASTED PORK
Bayerischer Krustenbraten

Serves 6 | **Prep time:** 20 minutes | **Cook time:** 1 hour 30 minutes to 2 hours

Does anything sound more German than tender, roasted pork with a crust of salty, fatty skin, served with a rich, beer-flavored gravy? This recipe takes time but not a lot of effort. Probably the hardest part is finding that perfect cut of meat. You'll need boneless pork shoulder roast with a nice layer of fat, and to get the "cracklings," it should have skin. If you're not comfortable deboning pork, just make friends with your butcher and let them do it.

---

1 (3½- to 4-pound) boneless, skin-on pork shoulder roast

3 teaspoons salt

2 teaspoons freshly ground black pepper

2 tablespoons butter

1 onion, chopped

3 or 4 carrots, chopped

3 parsnips, peeled and chopped

1 or 2 turnips, peeled and chopped

2 celery stalks, chopped

5 whole cloves

2 (12-ounce) bottles dark beer

1 cup water, plus 1 tablespoon

1 tablespoon cornstarch

1. Preheat the oven to 350°F.

2. Rinse and pat dry the pork with paper towels. Use a knife to score a diamond pattern into the skin. Rub the roast all over with the salt and pepper, making sure to get it into the cuts.

3. Melt the butter in a roasting pan over medium-high heat on the stovetop. Brown the roast all over, at least 3 minutes per side.

4. Roast in the oven for 30 minutes. Carefully remove from the oven, add the onion, carrots, parsnips, turnips, celery, and cloves and pour the beer over the roast. Return the pan to the oven and roast for at least 1 hour, or until a meat thermometer reads 150°F. Check occasionally and add water to the pan if it looks dry.

5. Cover with aluminum foil and let rest for 20 minutes.

6. Spoon the roasted vegetables onto a serving plate and cover to keep warm. Add 1 cup of water to the liquid in the pan and, using a wooden spoon, scrape up the browned bits. Strain the gravy into a saucepan and cook over medium heat until bubbling. In a small cup, mix the cornstarch with the remaining 1 tablespoon of water and whisk into the gravy. Cook, whisking constantly, until thickened.

7. Cut the meat into slices and transfer to the serving plate with the vegetables. Spoon some gravy over the top and serve the rest on the side.

ROASTED PORK HOCKS
Schweinshaxe

Serves 6 | **Prep time:** 15 minutes | **Cook time:** 3 hours 30 minutes

Juicy hocks with crispy, crackling skin—it's a scene straight out of Oktoberfest. Ask your butcher for pork hocks and not ham hocks (which are smoked).

3 bay leaves

1 teaspoon peppercorns

5 whole cloves

1 onion, quartered

2 garlic cloves, chopped

3 pork hocks

2 onions, sliced

1 (12-ounce) bottle beer

1 teaspoon ground caraway

2 to 3 teaspoons salt

1 teaspoon freshly ground
   black pepper

1 cup water, plus
   1 tablespoon

1 tablespoon cornstarch

1. Fill two-thirds of a large pot (big enough for all the hocks) with water. Add the bay leaves, peppercorns, cloves, the quartered onion, and garlic and bring to a boil over high heat. Turn the heat to medium-low, add the hocks, and cook for 1 hour.

2. Preheat the oven to 300°F. Put a rack in a roasting pan. Put the sliced onions and beer in the pan.

3. Remove the hocks from the water. Using a knife, score a diamond pattern into the skin. In a small bowl, mix together the caraway, salt, and pepper. Rub the seasonings into the hock skin.

4. Set the hocks on the roasting rack and roast for 1 hour. Turn the hocks and roast for another 1 hour. If the skin is getting too brown, cover with aluminum foil.

5. After 2 hours, raise the temperature to 400°F. Roast the hocks for 5 to 10 minutes, turning once or twice, until the skin is crispy. Remove the hocks.

6. Add 1 cup of water to the pan and scrape up the browned bits. Strain into a saucepan and cook over medium-high heat. In a cup, mix together the cornstarch and the remaining 1 tablespoon of water, then whisk the mixture into the drippings until thickened. Serve the hocks with the sauce on the side.

HAM AND NOODLES
Schinkennudeln

Serves 4 | **Prep time:** 20 minutes | **Cook time:** 25 minutes

Noodles fried in butter were one of the simple pleasures of my childhood. Schinkennudeln is pure comfort food, and it's also a way of using up leftover ham. I like to use wide egg noodles, while a friend swears by rotini, but most pastas will work.

Salt

1 pound pasta, any shape

3 tablespoons butter

1 onion, diced

12 to 16 ounces ham, diced

6 eggs

⅓ cup heavy
　(whipping) cream

½ teaspoon freshly ground
　black pepper

Chopped fresh chives
　(optional), for garnish

1. Bring a large pot of salted water to a boil over high heat and cook the pasta according to the package directions. Drain and set aside.

2. While the pasta is cooking, melt the butter in a large sauté pan or skillet over medium heat. Add the onion and ham and cook until the onion is soft. If it starts to turn brown, lower the heat.

3. Add the pasta to the ham and onion. Raise the heat a little bit and cook, stirring constantly, until you get a few browned edges.

4. In a small bowl, whisk together the eggs, cream, ½ teaspoon of salt, then pepper, and pour the mixture over the noodles. Stir until the eggs begin to set.

5. Sprinkle with the chives (if using) and serve.

VARIATION TIP: My American kids love to eat Schinkennudeln with ketchup (and, honestly, it's pretty good).

HAWAIIAN TOAST
Toast Hawaii

Serves 6 | **Prep time:** 10 minutes | **Cook time:** 5 to 10 minutes

5-INGREDIENT · 30-MINUTE

Hawaiian toast might seem like an odd thing to find in a German cookbook, but this simple comfort food has been a quick favorite in my family since the 1950s. Think of it as a jazzed-up grilled cheese sandwich. What's not to like? Gooey cheese, salty ham, and sweet tangy pineapple, all on a piece of buttered and toasted bread. In Germany, you would typically use Gruyère, Emmentaler, or Gouda cheese, but you can use Swiss as well.

6 tablespoons
  (¾ stick) butter

6 slices white bread

6 slices deli ham

6 slices canned pineapple

6 slices cheese

6 maraschino cherries
  (optional)

1. Preheat the oven to 350°F. Line a baking sheet with parchment paper.

2. Spread 1 tablespoon of butter evenly on one side of each slice of bread and place it on the prepared baking sheet, buttered side up. Top each with a slice of ham (folded if necessary), center a slice of pineapple on the ham, and top with a slice of cheese and a maraschino cherry (if using).

3. Bake for 5 to 10 minutes, or until the cheese is melted. Serve warm and gooey.

RUSTIC POTATO SOUP WITH SMOKED SAUSAGE
Kartoffelsuppe mit Mettwurst

Serves 6 | **Prep time:** 15 minutes | **Cook time:** 40 minutes

ONE-POT

This rustic potato soup, loaded with chunks of potato and slices of smoked sausage, will fill up even the hungriest teenager at your dinner table. Mettwurst, a smoked pork sausage, might be tough to find, but smoked pork kielbasa can easily be substituted. When I serve this soup at home, it's usually accompanied by a bottle of Maggi liquid seasoning, so people can add a little extra flavor.

2 tablespoons butter

1 yellow onion, diced

1 small leek, washed well, thinly sliced

2 celery stalks, diced

2 carrots, diced

6 cups water

3 pounds russet potatoes, peeled and diced

1 teaspoon dried thyme

2 lovage sprigs or celery greens sprigs, chopped

3 parsley sprigs, chopped, divided

1 teaspoon salt

1 teaspoon freshly ground black pepper

1 bouillon cube

1 pound mettwurst or smoked pork kielbasa sausage

1. Melt the butter in a large soup pot over medium-high heat. Add the onion, leek, celery, and carrots and cook for 3 to 4 minutes until soft. Add the water, potatoes, thyme, lovage, two-thirds of the parsley, salt, pepper, bouillon, and sausage. Stir until combined and bring to a boil.

2. Turn the heat to medium-low and simmer for about 30 minutes until the potatoes are easy to pierce with a knife.

3. Transfer the sausage to a cutting board and cut it into slices. Return the sausage to the soup, sprinkle with the remaining one-third of the parsley, and stir until combined. Serve hot.

VARIATION TIP: For a smoother soup, remove the sausage, purée the soup, then return the sausage to the pot. For a creamier soup, add heavy cream.

KALE SOUP WITH SAUSAGE
Grünkohlsuppe mit Wurst

Serves 6 | **Prep time:** 15 minutes | **Cook time:** 1 hour 5 minutes

ONE-POT

Germans were eating kale long before it was trendy in green smoothies and fancy salads. It would never occur to my Oma to eat it raw—she cooked and served it in a delicious stock that I swear could be sold as a beverage. This recipe traditionally uses pinkel sausage, which is difficult to find in the United States, but you can use smoked pork kielbasa, and it will taste wonderful.

2 tablespoons vegetable oil

1 yellow onion, diced

3 or 4 bacon slices, roughly diced

2 bunches curly kale, stemmed and leaves chopped

6 cups beef stock

1 pound smoked pork kielbasa

2 large russet potatoes, peeled and cut into 1-inch cubes

½ teaspoon ground nutmeg

Salt (optional)

Freshly ground black pepper (optional)

1. Heat the oil in a large soup pot over medium heat. Add the onion and bacon and cook for 4 to 5 minutes, stirring occasionally, until the onion is soft and the bacon has begun to render.

2. Add the kale and stock to the pot, stir until combined, and bring to a boil over medium-high heat. Turn the heat to low, add the sausage, cover, and cook for 30 minutes.

3. Transfer the sausage to a plate. Add the potatoes to the kale, stir, and cook for another 30 minutes.

4. Add the nutmeg and stir. Cut the sausage into slices and return it to the soup. Taste, and add salt and pepper, if needed.

PEA SOUP WITH HAM
Erbsensuppe

Serves 6 | **Prep time:** 20 minutes | **Cook time:** 1 hour 15 minutes

ONE-POT

Warm and satisfying, pea soup is a great way to feed a crowd on a cold day. This recipe is loaded with bacon and ham, and be sure to add a Wiener (frankfurter) for each person at the table (that's what my Oma would do).

---

4 bacon slices, chopped

1 large yellow onion, diced

2 large carrots, diced

1 small leek (white part only), washed well, thinly sliced

¼ knob celeriac or celery root, peeled and diced

2½ cups split peas, rinsed

1 smoked ham hock

2 bay leaves

1 teaspoon dried marjoram

1 bunch fresh parsley, chopped, divided

7 cups water

3 medium russet potatoes, peeled and diced

Salt (optional)

Freshly ground black pepper (optional)

6 frankfurters

1. In a large soup pot over medium heat, cook the bacon for about 2 minutes until it starts to brown. Add the onion and cook for 1 minute. Add the carrots, leek, and celeriac, stir, and cook for about 5 minutes until soft.

2. Add the split peas, ham hock, bay leaves, marjoram, half of the parsley, and water and bring to a boil over medium-high heat.

3. Turn the heat to medium-low, cover, and simmer for 30 minutes, stirring every 10 minutes to prevent sticking.

4. Add the potatoes and cook, stirring occasionally, for 25 minutes. Taste, and add salt and pepper, if needed.

5. Transfer the ham hock to a cutting board and cut off any meat that remains on the bone. Dice the meat and return it to the soup. Add the frankfurters and cook for 5 minutes. Spoon the soup into bowls, making sure each bowl has a frankfurter, and sprinkle with the remaining parsley.

Prussian Meatballs in White Caper Sauce *Königsberger Klopse*, p. 86

BEEF AND LAMB

GERMAN BEEF PATTIES
Frikadellen

Makes 6 patties | **Prep time:** 10 minutes | **Cook time:** 20 minutes

30-MINUTE

These moist and flavorful beef patties are sort of like a cross between a hamburger and a meatball. Frikadellen have different regional names across Germany, and everyone has their own seasoning twist. This recipe makes enough patties for six people (unless you happen to be my cousin, who once consumed eight in a single sitting). Serve these with potato salad or mashed potatoes with gravy or enjoy on a bun.

1 pound ground beef
8 ounces ground pork
1 cup bread crumbs
1 yellow onion, diced

2 eggs
1 teaspoon salt
1 teaspoon freshly ground
    black pepper

3 tablespoons chopped
    fresh parsley
Vegetable oil, for frying

1. In a large bowl, mix the ground beef, ground pork, bread crumbs, onion, eggs, salt, pepper, and parsley, using your hands or a wooden spoon.

2. Form the mixture into 6 patties, each about 1 inch thick and 4 inches wide.

3. Heat the oil in a large sauté pan or skillet over medium-high heat until the oil shimmers. Add the patties and cook for 2 minutes. Turn over the patties and cook for 2 more minutes. Turn the heat to medium-low and cook each side for an additional 7 minutes. Serve hot.

INGREDIENT TIP: This recipe does need some fat so it won't dry out. I find that 85% ground beef works best.

VARIATION TIP: If you don't have ground pork, you can make frikadellen using just beef. I won't tell. Or you change the flavor by adding 1 tablespoon of German mustard, 1 minced garlic clove, or 1 teaspoon of dried marjoram or paprika when you mix all the other ingredients.

STEAK WITH HERBED BUTTER
Steak mit Kräuterbutter

Serves 6 | **Prep time:** 10 minutes, plus 20 minutes to rest | **Cook time:** 15 minutes

5-INGREDIENT

A simple steak is elevated to fine dining when you top it with a pat of herbed butter after cooking. The butter adds extra richness to the meat, while the herbs offer a pop of fresh flavor.

6 (5- to 7-ounce) sirloin steaks

Salt

Freshly ground black pepper

1 cup (2 sticks) butter, plus 2 tablespoons, at room temperature

2 garlic cloves, crushed

2 tablespoons finely chopped fresh parsley

2 tablespoons finely chopped fresh chives

2 tablespoons vegetable oil

1. Generously season the steaks with salt and pepper and let them rest for 20 minutes before cooking.

2. In a medium bowl, mix together 1 cup of butter, garlic, parsley, and chives until completely combined. Add ½ teaspoon of salt, if using unsalted butter. Cover with plastic wrap and refrigerate until ready to use.

3. In a large sauté pan or skillet over medium-high heat, heat the oil and the remaining 2 tablespoons of butter until the butter melts and the oil shimmers. Add the steaks and cook for 4 minutes on each side. Spoon some of the steak juices and pan butter over the steaks. Cook an extra 2 minutes for medium, or more for your desired doneness.

4. Top each steak with a scoop of herbed butter and serve with more on the side.

PRUSSIAN MEATBALLS IN WHITE CAPER SAUCE
Königsberger Klopse

Makes 18 meatballs | **Prep time:** 30 minutes | **Cook time:** 40 minutes

These fabulous meatballs, served in a white caper sauce, get their name from the old Prussian capital, Königsberg. It's a meal Mom knew we would all race to the table for. As a child, I picked out the capers, but as an adult, I've come to really adore their salty-sour flavor. And, yes, anchovy paste goes into the meatballs. Trust me, you won't notice it's there, but you will notice if it isn't. Serve over boiled potatoes, mashed potatoes, or rice.

5 to 6 cups beef stock

1 bay leaf

3 or 4 peppercorns

2 slices white bread

⅓ cup milk

1 pound ground beef

8 ounces ground pork

1 egg

½ yellow onion,
   finely chopped

1 tablespoon anchovy paste

1 tablespoon chopped
   fresh parsley

½ teaspoon salt, plus more
   if needed

½ teaspoon freshly ground
   black pepper, plus more
   if needed

2 tablespoons
   capers, divided

2 tablespoons butter

2 tablespoons
   all-purpose flour

1 teaspoon freshly squeezed
   lemon juice

Pinch ground nutmeg

⅓ cup heavy
   (whipping) cream

1. In a large saucepan, mix together 5 cups of stock, the bay leaf, and peppercorns and bring to a boil over high heat. Turn the heat to medium-low and simmer for 5 minutes while you make the meatballs.

2. Tear the bread into small pieces, place them in a small bowl with the milk, and let soak.

3. In a large bowl, mix together the ground beef, ground pork, egg, onion, anchovy paste, parsley, salt, pepper, and 1 tablespoon of capers. Squeeze the milk out of the bread. Add the mushy bread to the meat mixture and mix and knead with your hands until completely combined.

4. Set a clean plate next to the bowl. Wet your hands. Using your hands, roll the meat mixture into 18 (2-inch) meatballs (about the size of a golf ball) and place them on the plate.

5. Using a slotted spoon, carefully drop the meatballs, one by one, into the simmering stock and gently stir so they don't get stuck together. If the stock doesn't cover them completely, add the remaining 1 cup of stock. Simmer, gently stirring occasionally, for 15 minutes.

6. Using the slotted spoon, transfer the meatballs to a bowl. Strain the stock into a large bowl and discard the bay leaf and peppercorns.

7. In the same saucepan, melt the butter over medium heat. Add the flour and whisk together to form a smooth paste. Add 2 cups of the strained stock and whisk until smooth and beginning to thicken. Add the remaining 1 tablespoon of capers, lemon juice, nutmeg, and cream. Taste, and add salt and pepper, if needed. Pour the sauce over the meatballs and serve.

CABBAGE ROLLS
Krautwickel/Kohlrouladen

Makes 12 cabbage rolls | **Prep time:** 45 minutes | **Cook time:** 1 hour 30 minutes

These cabbage rolls are an example of how "humble" food can be elevated to something amazingly delicious. Serve them with mashed potatoes.

Salt

1 head savoy cabbage, damaged outer leaves removed, cored

1½ pounds ground beef

½ yellow onion, finely diced

½ cup bread crumbs

1 egg

½ teaspoon dried thyme

½ teaspoon freshly ground black pepper

2 tablespoons butter, divided

2 tablespoons vegetable oil, divided

2 cups beef stock

1 teaspoon cornstarch

1 tablespoon water

1. Bring a large soup pot three-quarters full of salted water to a boil over high heat. Turn the heat to medium-low and simmer.

2. Lower the cabbage into the simmering water and cook for 4 to 5 minutes. Transfer the cabbage to a colander and let drain and cool for a few minutes.

3. In a medium bowl, mix together the ground beef, onion, bread crumbs, egg, thyme, 1 teaspoon of salt, and pepper with your hands until completely combined.

4. Peel off a leaf of cabbage and lay it on a cutting board with the stem end facing you. Put 2 to 3 tablespoons of the meat filling in the center of the leaf and fold it up like a small burrito. Secure the roll using kitchen twine or a toothpick. Repeat with the remaining leaves and filling.

5. In a large sauté pan or skillet with a lid, combine 1 tablespoon of butter and 1 tablespoon of oil over medium-high heat and stir until the butter is melted. Place about half of the cabbage rolls in the pan, making sure not to overcrowd them. Cook for 2 to 3 minutes per side until they brown. Transfer the rolls to a plate and repeat with the remaining 1 tablespoon of butter, the remaining 1 tablespoon of oil, and the remaining cabbage rolls.

6. Place all the cabbage rolls in the pan, pour in the stock and bring to a boil over medium-high heat. Turn the heat to medium-low, cover, and cook for 30 minutes. Flip over the rolls and let cook for another 30 minutes. Transfer the cabbage rolls to a serving platter.

7. In a cup, mix together the cornstarch and water. Add the mixture to the leftover juices in the pan and whisk over medium heat until thickened. Serve with the cabbage rolls.

BRAISED BEEF ROLLS
Rouladen

Serves 6 | **Prep time:** 30 minutes | **Cook time:** 2 hours

Rouladen is my number one requested recipe. Beef is rolled up with onion, pickles, bacon, and mustard, then braised until the meat is fall-apart tender. Serve with German Egg Noodles (page 35) or Potato Dumplings (page 37) and Red Cabbage (page 43).

6 (6- to 8-ounce) slices
 ¼-inch-thick flat top round
 or London broil
Salt
Freshly ground
 black pepper

4 to 5 teaspoons German or
 yellow mustard
4 bacon slices, diced
2 or 3 German pickles, diced
1 medium onion, diced
3 tablespoons vegetable oil

2 cups beef stock
2 tablespoons cornstarch
2 tablespoons water

1. Sprinkle each steak generously with salt and pepper and spread with mustard. Top each piece with equal amounts of bacon, pickles, and onion, spreading them out evenly over the meat.

2. Starting at one end, roll each slice into a roll and secure with a toothpick.

3. In a large sauté pan or skillet with a lid over medium-high heat, heat the oil until it shimmers. Add the rolls and cook, turning the rolls every 3 minutes until well browned on all sides.

4. Transfer the rolls to a plate. Add the stock to the pan, using a wooden spoon to scrape up any browned bits, and bring to a boil. Turn the heat to medium-low, return the rolls to the pan, cover, and simmer for 1½ hours.

5. Transfer the rolls to a plate. Raise the heat to medium-high and cook until the liquid bubbles. In a small bowl, whisk together the cornstarch and water, then whisk it into the pan liquid. Continue whisking until the sauce thickens.

6. Top the rolls with some sauce and serve the rest on the side.

BREADED VEAL CUTLETS
Wienerschnitzel

Serves 4 | **Prep time:** 10 minutes | **Cook time:** 20 minutes

5-INGREDIENT · 30-MINUTE

There are many schnitzel recipes, but a true Wienerschnitzel comes to you simply—breaded, fried, and served with a wedge of lemon. Traditionally, the dish is made from veal, but you can substitute pork or even turkey. Just make sure you use enough oil, which helps the Schnitzel stay tender.

4 (5- to 6-ounce) veal cutlets

Salt

Freshly ground
   black pepper

Vegetable oil, for frying

¾ cup all-purpose flour

2 eggs, beaten

¾ to 1 cup bread crumbs

Lemon wedges, for serving

1. Using a meat hammer, pound the cutlets to approximately ¼ inch thick. Season with salt and pepper.

2. Pour 1 inch of oil into a large sauté pan or skillet over medium-high heat, and heat oil to 350°F.

3. Put the flour in a small bowl, the beaten eggs in another small bowl, and the bread crumbs in a third small bowl. Dip a cutlet into the flour, coating both sides, and shake off any excess. Then, dip it into the eggs, coating both sides, and let the excess drip off. Finally, dip the cutlet into the bread crumbs, pressing them into the meat to make sure they stick.

4. Carefully slide the breaded cutlet into the oil. It should float in the oil and not touch the bottom of the pan. Cook for 2 to 3 minutes per side. Transfer to a platter lined with paper towels. Repeat with the remaining cutlets. Keep cutlets in the oven at a low temp to keep warm until ready to serve.

COOKING TIP: If your pan is big enough, you can cook multiple cutlets at one time—be careful not to overcrowd the pan.

MARINATED ROAST BEEF
Sauerbraten

Serves 6 | **Prep time:** 15 minutes, plus at least 3 days to marinate and 30 minutes to soak the raisins | **Cook time:** 2 hours 30 minutes to 3 hours

This Sauerbraten recipe requires a few days to make, but the result—tender meat loaded with flavors that explode in your mouth—is worth the wait. Pair it with Red Cabbage (page 43) and Potato Dumplings (page 37) or German Egg Noodles (page 35).

2 onions, thinly sliced

2 carrots, thinly sliced

4 bay leaves

7 or 8 juniper berries

5 whole cloves

5 allspice berries

3 garlic cloves, roughly chopped

1 teaspoon salt, plus more if needed

1 teaspoon freshly ground black pepper, plus more if needed

1 teaspoon sugar

1 cup red wine vinegar

3 cups red wine

1 (3- to 4-pound) beef roast, eye of round, or rump roast

Handful raisins

2 tablespoons vegetable oil

2 cups beef stock

2 tablespoons honey

2 slices pumpernickel bread

2 tablespoons cornstarch

2 tablespoons water

1. In a large bowl, mix together the onions, carrots, bay leaves, juniper berries, cloves, allspice berries, garlic, salt, pepper, sugar, vinegar, and wine until the sugar is dissolved. Pour the marinade into a large zip-top plastic bag and place the roast into the bag. Seal, place the bag into a large bowl, and refrigerate for at least 3 and up to 5 days, turning daily to make sure the meat is evenly coated.

2. On the day of serving, preheat the oven to 350°F.

3. In a small bowl of water, soak the raisins until plump, about 30 minutes. Remove the meat from the marinade. Strain the vegetables from the marinade and set both aside. Pat dry the meat with paper towels. Heat the oil in a Dutch oven or roasting pan with a lid over medium-high heat. Brown the meat, searing for at least 3 minutes on each side. Add the vegetables from the marinade, reserving the marinade, and cook for 3 to 4 minutes until browned. Add the stock, reserved marinade, honey, and bread.

4. Cover and roast for 2 hours. Check to see whether the meat is tender (it may need to cook longer if you have a larger roast). Transfer the meat to a cutting board, cover with aluminum foil to keep warm, and let rest.

5. Strain the juices from the Dutch oven into the pan and press the vegetables through the strainer. Cook the juices over medium-high heat until bubbling. Add the raisins. In a small cup, mix together the cornstarch and water, then add the mixture to the pan and whisk until the sauce thickens. Taste, and add more salt and pepper, if needed.

6. Cut the meat into slices and serve with the sauce.

FRANKISH BEEF ROAST WITH ONION SAUCE
Frankische Zwiebelfleisch

Serves 4 to 6 | **Prep time:** 30 minutes | **Cook time:** 2 hours

5-INGREDIENT · ONE-POT

Imagine you are in Upper Franconia, looking to duck out of the cold weather with a comforting meal in a cozy Gaststätte (tavern). This super tender and juicy roast beef dish would absolutely do the trick. Serve it with Potato Dumplings (page 37) to soak up every bit of the caramelized onion sauce.

2 tablespoons vegetable oil

1 (2½- to 3-pound) beef
  sirloin roast

2½ pounds onions, cut
  into rings

1½ tablespoons salt

1½ tablespoons freshly
  ground black pepper

1½ tablespoons paprika

1 cup white wine

3 cups beef stock, divided

1. Preheat the oven to 325°F.

2. Heat the oil in a Dutch oven over medium-high heat, until shimmering. Add the roast and brown all over, making sure to sear the ends as well as all the sides, about 3 minutes per side. Transfer the meat to a plate and set aside.

3. Add the onions to the Dutch oven and cook for 4 to 5 minutes, stirring often, until brown. Add the salt, pepper, paprika, and wine and stir, scraping up the browned bits from the bottom of the pan.

4. Return the meat to the Dutch oven on top of the onions and add 1½ cups of stock. Cover, place the pot in the oven, and bake for 15 minutes. Turn the meat over, stir the onions lightly, and add the remaining 1½ cups of stock. Cover and cook for 1 hour 15 minutes.

5. Transfer the roast to a plate and let rest a few minutes.

6. Cut the meat into slices, pour some of the onion sauce over the meat, and serve the rest of the sauce on the side.

CORNED BEEF HASH WITH BEETS
Labskaus

Serves 4 | **Prep time:** 45 minutes | **Cook time:** 15 minutes

German sailors often ate Labskaus because the corned beef traveled well. Of course, they added a twist: pickled beets and marinated herring. Today, the dish is still popular in Bremen and has a reputation as an effective hangover cure. (Not that I'd know anything about that . . .)

4 to 6 pickled beets, liquid
  reserved

4 large russet potatoes,
  boiled, peeled, and cut
  into 1-inch chunks

1 cup beef stock

2 tablespoons vegetable oil

1 onion, diced

12 ounces canned corned
  beef, diced

Salt

Freshly ground
  black pepper

2 tablespoons butter

4 eggs

Pickled herring, for serving

German pickles, for serving

1. Dice 2 of the beets, cut the rest into slices, and set aside.

2. In a large bowl, combine the potatoes and stock and smash the potatoes with a potato masher. You want them mashed but still chunky. Set aside.

3. Heat the oil in a large sauté pan or skillet over medium-high heat. Add the onion and cook for about 4 minutes, stirring, until translucent. Add the corned beef and cook, stirring often, for 3 minutes. Add the diced beets and cook, stirring, for 1 minute. Add the smashed potatoes, salt and pepper to taste, and a few tablespoons of the reserved beet liquid and stir until combined. Set aside.

4. Melt the butter in another sauté pan or skillet over medium heat. Crack the eggs into the pan. Cook for about 3 minutes until the egg whites are no longer clear. Flip over the eggs and cook for 30 seconds longer.

5. Divide the hash onto 4 plates and top each with a fried egg. Season the eggs with salt and pepper, if needed. Serve with the sliced beets, herring, and pickles on the side.

"FALSE RABBIT" MEATLOAF WITH EGG
Falscher Hase

Serves 6 | **Prep time:** 20 minutes | **Cook time:** 1 hour

The name of this dish dates back to a time when rabbit roasts were hard to get. Cooks would shape a meatloaf of ground meat into a vaguely rabbit-like shape. When the meatloaf is sliced, the hidden eggs make this dish look Instagram perfect. Leftovers make a terrific sandwich filling.

6 eggs

1 pound ground beef

8 ounces ground pork

1 cup bread crumbs

1 teaspoon salt

1 teaspoon freshly ground black pepper

½ teaspoon ground nutmeg

1 small onion, diced

2 tablespoons chopped fresh parsley

2 teaspoons mustard

1½ cups beef stock

1 to 2 tablespoons cornstarch

3 tablespoons water

1. Preheat the oven to 350°F.

2. Fill a small saucepan with water and place it on the stovetop over high heat. Using a needle or tack, carefully poke a small hole in the fat bottom end of 4 eggs. Place the eggs into the saucepan and bring to a boil. Turn the heat to low and simmer for 10 minutes until the eggs are hard-boiled. Drain the boiling water, and run cold water into the pan to stop the cooking. Peel the eggs and set aside.

3. In a large bowl, mix together the ground beef, ground pork, remaining 2 eggs, bread crumbs, salt, pepper, nutmeg, onion, parsley, and mustard, using your hands to mix everything well.

4. Spread a quarter of the meat mixture into the bottom of a 9-by-5-inch loaf pan. Put the hard-boiled eggs end to end on top of the meat, so that they run lengthwise down the center of the pan. Fill the pan with the remaining meat mixture, making sure to fill around the eggs. Smooth the top of the loaf and bake for 45 minutes. Remove loaf from the pan and let rest.

5. Using a wooden spoon, scrape up any browned bits and drippings from the loaf pan into a saucepan. Add the stock and bring to a boil over medium-high heat. In a small cup, mix together the cornstarch and water, then whisk the mixture into the stock, and cook, whisking often, until thickened.

6. Cut the meatloaf into slices and serve with the sauce.

GROUND BEEF SAUCE
Haschee

Serves 4 | **Prep time:** 5 minutes | **Cook time:** 25 minutes

30-MINUTE

After a long day of travel, my aunt would serve me a plate of Haschee, the ultimate comfort food. It's a simple dish—ground beef cooked with onions and mushrooms—but it's loaded with meaty flavor. Many regions (and everyone's aunt) have slightly different seasoning additions. This version uses paprika, but some Germans might remember it with allspice. Serve it over rice or mashed potatoes.

1 tablespoon vegetable oil

1 large onion, diced

1½ pounds ground beef

1½ cups mushrooms, sliced

2 cups beef stock

½ teaspoon salt

½ teaspoon freshly ground
  black pepper

1 teaspoon paprika

1 teaspoon mustard

1 tablespoon cornstarch

1 tablespoon water

1. In a sauté pan or skillet, heat the oil over medium heat. Add the onion and cook for 3 to 4 minutes until translucent and soft. Add the ground beef and cook for about 5 minutes, stirring frequently to break up any lumps, until brown and crumbled. Add the mushrooms and cook for 1 minute.

2. Add the stock, salt, pepper, paprika, and mustard and cook for about 15 minutes, stirring often, until the flavors blend.

3. In a cup, mix together the cornstarch and water, then add the cornstarch mixture to the meat mixture and cook for 3 to 4 minutes until the sauce is thickened.

ROLLED LAMB ROAST
Lammrollbraten

Serves 6 | **Prep time:** 30 minutes | **Cook time:** 1 hour 45 minutes

Easter in Germany means eggs, bunnies, and lamb, so, like many German families, on Easter we traditionally enjoy roast lamb. (Don't tell my Oma. She always swore she hated lamb, so my aunt would tell her we were enjoying beef.) This recipe does require a little extra preparation because of the rolling and tying, but you can take care of this ahead of time. Serve with roasted potatoes, Green Beans with Bacon (page 42), or asparagus.

1 (2½- to 3-pound) boneless leg of lamb

Salt

Freshly ground black pepper

5 to 6 tablespoons chopped fresh parsley

2 onions, diced, divided

3 garlic cloves

7 tablespoons olive oil, divided

2 tablespoons mustard

6 tablespoons fresh rosemary, or

4 tablespoons dried rosemary, divided

2 tablespoons chopped fresh thyme, or

1 tablespoon dried thyme

¾ cup red wine

2 cups vegetable stock

1. Trim the lamb of any fat pockets, silver skin, and tendons. Season liberally with salt and pepper.

2. Preheat the oven to 350°F.

3. In a food processor, combine the parsley, 1 diced onion, garlic, 4 tablespoons of oil, mustard, and half of the rosemary and pulse until finely chopped. Spread the herb filling over the lamb. Starting at the short end of the roast, roll up the lamb and tie it together with kitchen twine. Rub the outside with the thyme and the remaining half of the rosemary and season with salt and pepper.

4. Heat the remaining 3 tablespoons of oil in a roasting pan over medium heat on the stovetop. Add the remaining 1 diced onion and cook for about 4 minutes until translucent. Add the wine, stir to deglaze the pan, and add the stock.

CONTINUED >

5. Set the lamb roast into the pan and roast in the oven for 1 hour 10 minutes to 1 hour 20 minutes until the interior temperature reaches 125°F (for rare). Cover with aluminum foil and let rest for 10 to 15 minutes while you make the gravy.

6. Scrape up any brown bits in the pan. Pour the liquid into a clear measuring cup and let sit for a moment until the fat rises to the top. Pour off as much of the fat as you can. Pour the liquid into a blender and blend until smooth. Transfer the liquid to a saucepan and cook over medium-high until heated through. Taste and add salt and pepper, if needed.

7. Cut the lamb into slices, drizzle with some sauce, and serve the remaining sauce in a bowl at the table.

GOULASH SOUP
Goulaschsuppe

Serves 6 | **Prep time:** 15 minutes | **Cook time:** 2 hours

ONE-POT

Goulash soup appears on menus all over Germany once the weather turns cooler. Some versions are smoother, but I prefer my mother's hearty version with chunks of beef, carrot, and potato.

2 tablespoons butter

1 medium yellow onion, diced

1½ tablespoons Hungarian sweet paprika

1 teaspoon salt

1 teaspoon freshly ground black pepper

2 tablespoons tomato paste

1 tablespoon water, plus more if needed

1½ pounds beef stew meat, cut into 1-inch cubes

1 large carrot, thinly sliced

1 garlic clove, chopped

¾ teaspoon caraway seeds

½ teaspoon dried marjoram

3 large russet potatoes, peeled and cubed

5 cups beef stock

1. Melt the butter in a large Dutch oven over medium heat. Add the onion and cook for about 4 minutes until soft and translucent. Remove the pan from the heat and stir in the paprika, salt, pepper, tomato paste, and water. Add the beef, carrot, garlic, caraway seeds, and marjoram and stir until combined.

2. Return the Dutch oven to medium-high heat and cook until the meat begins to brown. Turn the heat to low, cover, and simmer, stirring often, for 1¼ hours. Check occasionally and add ¼ cup of water if it looks too dry.

3. Add the potatoes and stock and stir until combined. Simmer, partially covered, for about 30 minutes, until the potatoes are tender. Spoon into bowls and serve with a slice of rye bread and butter.

COOKING TIP: This soup tastes even better after a night in the refrigerator, so make it in advance for the best flavor.

GREEN BEAN SOUP
Grüne Bohneneintopf

Serves 6 | **Prep time:** 20 minutes | **Cook time:** 1 hour

This soup is served in many German households, and it's a huge favorite in our home as well. In Germany, it's traditionally seasoned with summer savory, but since I can't always find this herb in my grocery store, I use thyme instead.

3 tablespoons vegetable oil

1 pound lamb stew meat, cubed

1 medium onion, diced

2 teaspoons dried summer savory or thyme

Salt

Freshly ground black pepper

2 pounds green beans, trimmed and cut into 1- to 2-inch pieces

5 cups beef stock

1 pound potatoes, peeled and diced

3 bacon slices, chopped

1. Heat the oil in a large soup pot over medium-high heat. Add the lamb and cook for about 3 minutes on each side until browned. Add the onion and cook for about 4 minutes, stirring often, until translucent. Add the summer savory, season with salt and pepper, and stir until combined. Turn the heat to low, cover, and cook for 10 minutes.

2. Add the beans and stock to the pot, raise the heat to medium-high, and bring to a boil. Turn the heat to medium-low, cover, and simmer for 10 minutes.

3. Add the potatoes and cook for 20 minutes, or until the potatoes are tender.

4. In a small skillet over medium heat, fry the bacon until browned. Then, add the bacon and bacon fat to the soup. Taste and add more salt and pepper, if needed before serving.

COOKING TIP: You can have this soup ready in 35 minutes if you use ground beef and frozen green beans. Just brown the ground beef in the pot and add the thawed beans and potatoes when you would add fresh. Cook for 20 minutes, until the flavors come together.

SAUERKRAUT SOUP
Sauerkrautsuppe

Serves 6 to 8 | **Prep time:** 15 minutes | **Cook time:** 1 hour

ONE-POT

When I was growing up, I had never heard of sauerkraut soup. To me, sauerkraut was always a side dish. But I get asked a lot for this recipe, so I reached out to my friend Angela from All Tastes Germany, who is an amazing chef. She shared this easy recipe with me, and this rich flavorful soup has become a hit in our house. It's best served with slices of hearty rye bread and butter.

1 pound ground beef

1 (6-ounce) can tomato paste

2 onions, diced

1 (24-ounce) jar sauerkraut, drained and rinsed

8 bread-and-butter pickles, diced

1 teaspoon caraway seeds

2 cups white wine

4 cups beef stock

Salt (optional)

Freshly ground black pepper (optional)

1 cup sour cream

1. In a large soup pot or Dutch oven, cook the ground beef over medium heat for about 10 minutes until browned. Drain off any excess fat.

2. Add the tomato paste and cook, stirring, for 3 minutes. Add the onions, sauerkraut, pickles, and caraway seeds and stir until combined.

3. Add the wine and stock, raise the heat to medium-high, and bring to a boil. Turn the heat to medium-low and simmer for 45 minutes. Taste and add salt and pepper, if needed. Serve with dollops of sour cream.

Husum-Style Shrimp Salad *Husumer Krabbensalat*, p. 115

SEAFOOD

FISH PATTIES
Fischfrikadellen

Serves 4 to 6 | **Prep time:** 20 minutes | **Cook time:** 20 minutes

In our house we serve these fish patties with a simple remoulade, a salad, and a side of fries. Almost any fish will work for this recipe—salmon, cod, or even tilapia. Just don't skimp on the fresh herbs. Serve the patties on buns if you like.

FOR THE REMOULADE

½ cup mayonnaise
1 teaspoon mustard
½ pickle, chopped
½ teaspoon paprika
½ teaspoon freshly ground
   black pepper
1 tablespoon freshly
   squeezed lemon juice

FOR THE FISH PATTIES

1½ pounds fish fillets,
   skinned and boned
½ onion, diced
1 garlic clove, chopped
¼ cup chopped
   fresh parsley
¼ cup chopped fresh dill
2 eggs

1 cup bread crumbs
1 teaspoon salt
1 teaspoon freshly ground
   black pepper
4 tablespoons
   (½ stick) butter
Lemon wedges, for serving

TO MAKE THE REMOULADE

1. In a bowl, mix together the mayonnaise, mustard, pickle, paprika, pepper, and lemon juice and set aside.

TO MAKE THE FISH PATTIES

2. Using a food processor, meat grinder, or sharp knife, chop the fish until it has the texture of ground beef (a few chunks are okay).

3. Transfer the fish to a large bowl. Add the onion, garlic, parsley, dill, eggs, bread crumbs, salt, and pepper and, using your hands, mix until well combined. Form the mixture into 6 or 7 patties about 1 inch thick and 4 inches wide.

4. Melt the butter in a large sauté pan or skillet over medium heat. Add the fish patties and cook for 5 minutes on each side. Turn the patties and cook again for 3 to 4 minutes on each side until the patties are browned but not dark. Serve with the lemon wedges and the remoulade.

BEER-BATTERED FISH
Backfisch

Serves 6 | **Prep time:** 20 minutes | **Cook time:** 20 to 30 minutes

5-INGREDIENT

Sure, fish is great, but it's the beer batter that makes this recipe crispy, flavorful, and absolutely awesome. As the chef, I happily do a little "quality control" in the kitchen, eating the crispy bits that might accidentally fall off the pieces as they come out of the oil. In Germany, Backfisch is often served on a roll with some remoulade (see page 106), or you can serve it with your favorite potato salad.

1½ pounds cod fillets

Salt

1¾ cups all-purpose flour

3 eggs

1 cup Helles or any pale
 lager beer

Vegetable oil, for frying

Lemon wedges, for serving

1. Rinse and pat dry the fish fillets with paper towels. Lightly season them with salt.

2. In a medium bowl, whisk together the flour and eggs. While whisking, slowly add the beer and keep whisking until smooth.

3. Pour 1 inch of oil into a deep fryer or a skillet over medium heat and heat it to 350°F. Set a plate covered with paper towels nearby.

4. One at a time, dip the fish fillets into the batter and slide them into the hot oil. Don't overcrowd the pan. Fry for 3 minutes on each side. Turn the fish again and fry each side for 1 minute until golden brown. Using tongs, transfer the fish to the paper towels and let rest for 1 minute. Serve with the lemon wedges.

COOKING TIP: If you are making a large amount of this recipe, you can keep the fillets warm in the oven. Set the oven to 250°F. Cover a baking sheet with paper towels and place a cooling rack over the paper towels. As the fish comes out of the oil, set it on the cooling rack in the oven to keep warm.

VARIATION TIP: Try different kinds of fish, like halibut, snapper, or any white-fleshed fish.

COD WITH MUSTARD SAUCE
Kabbeljau mit Senfsoße

Serves 4 | **Prep time:** 5 minutes | **Cook time:** 25 minutes

30-MINUTE

As with many German dishes, this recipe is as much about the sauce as the protein. The creamy mustard sauce has just enough bite without being over-whelming, which means you can substitute any fish you find on sale, and the result will be delicious. German mustard is ideal, but regular yellow mustard or even Dijon will work. Serve with parsley potatoes or even rice.

FOR THE COD

1½ pounds cod

¼ cup freshly squeezed
   lemon juice

Salt

2 tablespoons
   all-purpose flour

Vegetable oil, for frying

FOR THE MUSTARD SAUCE

2 tablespoons butter

1 tablespoon
   all-purpose flour

2 tablespoons mustard

½ cup milk

½ cup heavy
   (whipping) cream

2 tablespoons white wine
   or freshly squeezed
   lemon juice

Salt

TO MAKE THE COD

1. Cut the fish into 4 equal pieces. Sprinkle with the lemon juice, then season with salt on both sides. Dust both sides with flour.

2. Heat the oil in a large sauté pan or skillet over medium-high heat until it shimmers. Place the fish pieces in the pan and fry for 4 to 5 minutes on each side until the fish is cooked through and flaky. Set aside on a plate.

TO MAKE THE MUSTARD SAUCE

3. Melt the butter in a small saucepan over medium heat. Add the flour and whisk until smooth. Add the mustard, milk, and cream. Continue whisking until the mixture begins to thicken. Add the wine and whisk until combined. Taste and add salt, if needed. Continue to cook for 3 to 4 minutes, whisking constantly, until thickened.

4. Serve the fish with a spoonful of sauce over each piece, passing the rest of the sauce at the table.

VARIATION TIP: Try adding chopped fresh dill or parsley to the sauce for some extra flavor.

PAN-FRIED TROUT
Forelle nach Müllerinart

Serves 4 | **Prep time:** 10 minutes | **Cook time:** 20 minutes

5-INGREDIENT · 30-MINUTE

Friday night at our house was generally fish night, and this simple dish came to the table most often. Müllerinart means "how the miller's wife would make it." Presumably, she had flour, so she'd put a light breading on the fish, pan-fry it in a bit of butter, and pour the butter over the fish. Generally, this dish is made with trout, but I also love it with red snapper. Serve with rice or potatoes.

4 trout fillets, boned
Salt
Freshly ground
    black pepper

6 tablespoons (¾ stick)
    butter, divided
¼ cup all-purpose flour

Chopped fresh parsley, for
    garnish (optional)
Lemon wedges, for serving

1. Rinse the fish fillets and pat dry with paper towels. Season the fillets with salt and pepper on both sides.

2. Melt 3 tablespoons of butter in a large sauté pan or skillet over medium heat. Place a plate with the flour near the pan. Dredge the salted fillets in the flour, shake off any excess, and place in the pan. Cook for 5 to 8 minutes on each side until the fish easily flakes when you cut it with a spatula. Transfer the fish to a serving plate and sprinkle with the parsley (if using).

3. Melt the remaining 3 tablespoons of butter in the pan, using a wooden spoon to scrape up any browned bits. Pour some of the sauce over the fish and pass the rest at the table. Serve the lemon wedges on the side for squeezing.

VARIATION TIP: Put ½ cup bread crumbs on a second plate. After dipping the fish in the flour, dip it in the bread crumbs and fry as instructed.

SKEWERED GRILLED FISH
Steckerlfisch

Serves 6 | **Prep time:** 30 minutes | **Cook time:** 25 minutes

Outside the beer tents during summer and fall German festivals, you'll see whole fish on skewers grilling over open coals. They're best cooked over a campfire, but I use a grill for this recipe. You'll need wooden skewers that are long enough to rest on the sides of the grill or fire pit.

1 cup vegetable oil

½ cup chopped fresh thyme

½ cup chopped fresh rosemary

½ cup chopped fresh parsley

½ cup chopped fresh sage

6 whole mackerel or trout, cleaned with head and tail on

Juice of 1 lemon

Salt

Freshly ground black pepper

Lemon wedges, for serving

1. In a small bowl, mix together the oil, thyme, rosemary, parsley, and sage and set aside to let the herbs flavor the oil.

2. Prep a grill or fire pit for indirect heat. If using coals, they should be hot but not flaming.

3. Season the fish, first rubbing it with the lemon juice and then sprinkling it with salt and pepper both outside and inside the cavity. Coat the outside and inside of the fish with the herb mixture, using a basting brush to make sure the inner cavity is well coated. If there are herbs left over, tuck them inside the fish.

4. Insert long wooden skewers head-to-tail through the fish. If the skewers are thin, use two. Lay the skewers across the grill or over the fire pit.

5. Cook for 7 to 10 minutes per side. Rotate the skewers to cook the other side, then rotate them again to cook the belly, 15 to 25 minutes total. The skin should be crispy and the fish will look opaque.

6. Serve each whole fish with a lemon wedge.

FLATFISH WITH BACON
Scholle nach Finkenwerder Art

Serves 4 | **Prep time:** 15 minutes | **Cook time:** 20 minutes

This fish dish gets its name from Finkenwerder, an island in the Elbe River. Scholle, or Plaice, is a flatfish that isn't always easy to find in the United States. Luckily, you can substitute sole or flounder or any other flatfish. Don't forget the bacon—it's a great lure for the non–fish lovers in your life. The Finkenwerders traditionally served this recipe with boiled potatoes and a nice green salad, accompanied by a glass of white wine.

¼ cup vegetable oil
1 small onion, diced
4 to 6 lean bacon
 slices, diced

¼ cup all-purpose flour
4 (8- to 10-ounce) plaice,
 flounder, or sole fillets
Salt

6 tablespoons
 (¾ stick) butter
6 tablespoons chopped
 fresh parsley

1. Heat the oil in a sauté pan or skillet over medium heat. Add the onion and bacon and cook for 4 to 5 minutes, stirring often, until the onion is translucent and the bacon fat renders. Transfer the bacon and onion to a bowl and set aside.

2. Put the flour on a plate. Season the fish fillets with salt. Dredge the fillets lightly in the flour, shaking off any excess. Place the fillets in the pan skin-side up and cook for 4 minutes. Flip over the fillets and cook skin-side down for 4 to 5 minutes.

3. Add the butter to the pan and let it melt. Spoon the melted butter over the fish. The fish should be done when it flakes easily with a fork.

4. Transfer the fish to a serving platter. Drizzle with the melted butter from the pan and top with the bacon and onion. Sprinkle with the fresh parsley for serving.

COOKING TIP: If you don't have a pan large enough to cook 4 pieces of fish, use 2 pans and cook the fish at the same time.

SALMON WITH DILL SAUCE AND POTATOES

Lachs mit Dillsoße und Petersilienkartoffeln

Serves 6 | **Prep time:** 50 minutes | **Cook time:** 20 minutes

On a hot day, this salmon recipe will satisfy your appetite without feeling too heavy. The secret is the flavorful, fresh dill sauce, which is much lighter than many German sauces.

4 tablespoons (½ stick) butter, divided

1 tablespoon all-purpose flour

1 cup milk

4 tablespoons chopped fresh dill, divided

1 tablespoon freshly squeezed lemon juice

Salt

1½ pounds baby potatoes, boiled and kept warm

3 tablespoons chopped fresh parsley

1½ to 1¾ pounds salmon fillets

1 tablespoon vegetable oil

Freshly ground black pepper

1. Preheat the oven to 400°F.

2. In a small saucepan over medium heat, melt 2 tablespoons of butter. Whisk in the flour until smooth. Add the milk and whisk until the sauce just comes to a boil. Remove from the heat and whisk in 2 tablespoons of dill and the lemon juice. Taste and add salt, if needed. Set aside.

3. Place the potatoes in a large saucepan over low heat. Add the remaining 2 tablespoons of butter, parsley, and ½ teaspoon of salt and stir until combined.

4. Rinse and dry the fillets and remove any bones. Pour the oil into a baking pan. Season the salmon with salt and pepper and place the fillets in the baking pan skin-side down. Sprinkle with the remaining 2 tablespoons of dill and bake for 5 minutes per half inch of thickness, or until the fish flakes easily with a fork. Serve with the dill sauce.

HERRING SALAD
Heringsalat

Serves 4 | **Prep time:** 20 minutes

30-MINUTE · NO-COOK · ONE-POT

Traditionally Heringsalat gets served on New Year's Eve in Germany, but my mother prefers to serve it as a cool dish in the summer. Fans of this herring recipe can't get enough, but those less familiar may find the brilliant pink hue of this "fish salad" a bit odd at first. But it's delicious, and you should try it. Serve it with boiled potatoes, sliced hard-boiled eggs, or bread. Who knows? The pink might grow on you!

½ cup sour cream

3 tablespoons mayonnaise

½ medium onion, diced

6 ounces canned beets, diced

3 German pickles, diced

1 tablespoon pickle juice, from the jar

1 apple, peeled and diced (optional)

½ teaspoon salt, plus more as needed

½ teaspoon freshly ground black pepper, plus more as needed

2 (12-ounce) jars marinated herring, drained

1. In a medium bowl, mix together the sour cream, mayonnaise, onion, beets, pickles, pickle juice, apple (if using) salt, and pepper. Taste and add more seasoning, if needed.

2. Add the herring and carefully stir until combined.

VARIATION TIP: Add 2 cups boiled potatoes to the salad to make a heartier, more filling meal. You can also add hard-boiled egg slices.

HUSUM-STYLE SHRIMP SALAD
Husumer Krabbensalat

Serves 4 | **Prep time:** 20 minutes

5-INGREDIENT · 30-MINUTE · NO-COOK · ONE-POT

Northern Germany loves its seafood, especially in coastal cities such as Husum. Brown shrimp, Krabben *in German, turn up everywhere, especially on Brötchen (bread rolls) or in salads. This simple salad recipe using easy-to-find bay shrimp is as fresh and delicious as it comes, but you can also use it as a starting place and add more vegetables if you like. Serve the salad on lettuce, in a hollowed-out tomato, on half an avocado, or on a bun.*

2 tablespoons olive oil

3 tablespoons chopped fresh chives

3 tablespoons chopped fresh dill

Juice of 1 lemon

1 pound cooked bay shrimp

½ teaspoon salt, plus more if needed

½ teaspoon freshly ground black pepper

½ cup diced cucumber

In a medium bowl, mix together the oil, chives, and dill until combined. Add the lemon juice, shrimp, salt, and pepper and stir until combined. Add the cucumber and stir. Let sit for 10 minutes to let the flavors meld. Taste, and add more salt, if needed. Serve immediately.

VARIATION TIP: I prefer to use chives instead of onion, because I think the chives make the lemon and shrimp flavors shine, but you can dice half a red onion instead if you like. You can also add diced radishes or diced tomatoes to the shrimp.

Plum Cake with Streusel *Pflaumenkuchen/Zwetschenkuchen mit Streusel*, p. 122

DESSERTS

RED BERRY PUDDING
Rote Grütze

Serves 6 | **Prep time:** 10 minutes | **Cook time:** 20 minutes

5-INGREDIENT · 30-MINUTE · VEGAN

Rote Grütze is like a pudding, but not like the one you got in the school cafeteria. Thick and fruity, not super sweet, it's traditionally made with red currants, but raspberries work, too. This dish tastes great on its own but is best served with whipped cream or vanilla pudding or over Milk Rice (page 119).

6 cups fresh red currants or raspberries

¼ cup sugar

1 cup raspberry juice, divided

⅓ cup cornstarch

1 tablespoon freshly squeezed lemon juice

1. Combine the currants, sugar, and ½ cup of raspberry juice in a large saucepan and cook over medium heat for 3 to 5 minutes until the berries start to break down.

2. In a measuring cup, mix together the cornstarch and remaining ½ cup of juice. Stir half of the cornstarch juice into the currant mixture. The mixture will look hazy; continue to stir until the juice is clear. Bring the mixture to a boil. Stir in the rest of the cornstarch juice and cook for 2 to 3 minutes until the pudding thickens. Add the lemon juice, stir, and serve.

VARIATION TIP: Feel free to try different red berries or a mix, like a strawberry, blackberry, and raspberry combination. This recipe also works really well with frozen berries: Let them thaw first, and use the juice from the berries as well as the extra juice. If you have a real sweet tooth, add a bit more sugar.

MILK RICE (RICE PUDDING)
Milchreis

Serves 6 | **Prep time:** 5 minutes | **Cook time:** 35 minutes

5-INGREDIENT · VEGETARIAN

Warm, creamy, lightly sweetened rice pudding flavored with vanilla and topped with cinnamon sugar, Milchreis is a soothing comfort food. In Germany, it is sometimes served as a warm meal, almost like a sweet risotto, but generally you will find it enjoyed as dessert. I love it topped with fruit, and it's especially delicious with Red Berry Pudding (page 118) and some fresh fruit.

1 cup short-grain rice
1¼ cups sugar, divided
¼ teaspoon salt

4 cups whole milk, plus more if needed
1 teaspoon vanilla extract

1 tablespoon ground cinnamon

1. In a large saucepan, mix together the rice, 1 cup of sugar, and the salt. Add the milk and vanilla and bring to a boil, stirring often, over medium heat. Turn the heat to low and cook for about 25 minutes, stirring frequently, until the rice has absorbed all the milk.

2. Taste, and if it's not cooked through, add more milk and cook, stirring often, for 5 more minutes.

3. While the rice is cooking, mix the remaining ¼ cup of sugar and the cinnamon in a small bowl. Once the rice is done, sprinkle the cinnamon sugar over the rice pudding and serve immediately.

LEFTOVERS TIP: Milchreis tastes good when cooled, but it tends to lose its soft texture. To reheat it, add some milk, stir, and heat over medium heat until warmed through.

RHUBARB COMPOTE
Rhabarberkompott

Makes 3½ cups | **Prep time:** 10 minutes | **Cook time:** 20 minutes

5-INGREDIENT · 30-MINUTE · ONE-POT · VEGAN

This funky, super-tart vegetable turns up a lot in German baking, but I happen to like it best as a compote. Raw rhubarb is not tasty, but when you cook it with some sugar, it becomes a delightful sweet-tart pudding-like mixture. Serve it topped with whipped cream, or spoon it over vanilla pudding, ice cream, yogurt, or waffles.

---

1 pound rhubarb

⅓ cup sugar, plus more as needed

1 teaspoon vanilla extract

¼ cup water

2 tablespoons freshly squeezed lemon juice (optional)

1. Trim the ends and any leaves off the rhubarb and cut the stalks into 1-inch chunks. In a saucepan, mix together the rhubarb, sugar, vanilla, and water and cook over medium-high heat until the sugar dissolves and the mixture comes to a boil.

2. Turn the heat to medium-low and simmer for about 10 minutes, stirring occasionally, until the rhubarb is softened and starting to fall apart. Taste, and add more sugar, if needed. If it's too sweet, add the lemon juice.

3. Remove from the heat and let sit for a few minutes. Serve immediately or refrigerate for up to 3 days.

VARIATION TIP: Other fruits can be made into compote using the same technique but will require less sugar. Try making it with berries, peaches, or apricots and adjust the sugar to your taste.

SUNKEN APPLE CAKE
Versunkener Apfelkuchen

Serves 12 | **Prep time:** 10 minutes | **Cook time:** 45 minutes

VEGETARIAN

Most German home bakers have at least three different recipes for apple cake, depending on the occasion. Versunkener Apfelkuchen might be the most traditional, and it's also the least fussy.

---

10 tablespoons (1¼ sticks) butter, plus more for greasing the pan
3 or 4 tart, firm apples, peeled, quartered, and cored

Juice of 1 small lemon
¾ cup granulated sugar
Grated zest of 1 small lemon
1 teaspoon vanilla extract
3 eggs
1½ cups all-purpose flour

2 teaspoons baking powder
2 tablespoons milk
¼ cup powdered sugar

1. Preheat the oven to 350°F. Grease a 9-inch springform pan with butter. Score each apple quarter on the curved side, making slices every ¼ inch, but don't cut all the way through. Put all the apples in a bowl and sprinkle with the lemon juice.

2. In a stand mixer fitted with the paddle attachment, combine the butter, sugar, and lemon zest. Beat on medium speed for about 5 minutes until light and fluffy, scraping the bowl as needed. Add the vanilla and the eggs, one at a time, beating between each addition.

3. In another bowl, mix together the flour and baking powder, then add it slowly to the batter, alternating with the milk and beating until combined. Scrape down the bowl one more time to make sure all the flour is mixed in.

4. Spread the batter evenly into the prepared springform pan. Lay the apple quarters on top of the batter, placing one in the center and then putting the other apples around in a decorative pattern.

5. Bake for 40 to 45 minutes, or until a toothpick inserted into the center comes out clean. Let sit on a cooling rack until completely cool. Sprinkle with the powdered sugar just before serving.

PLUM CAKE WITH STREUSEL
Pflaumenkuchen/Zwetschenkuchen mit Streusel

Serves 12 | **Prep time:** 25 minutes | **Cook time:** 55 minutes

VEGETARIAN

Germans do love their Kaffeeklatsch, the afternoon time for a chat with friends over coffee and cake. During the summer it is virtually impossible to attend one without eating some Pflaumenkuchen, a sweet cake with tart, juicy plums and a crunchy streusel topping.

12 tablespoons (1½ sticks) butter, divided, plus more for greasing the pan

2 pounds firm plums

¾ cup sugar, divided

1 teaspoon grated lemon zest

2 eggs

2½ cups all-purpose flour, divided

1 teaspoon baking powder

2 tablespoons instant vanilla pudding powder, divided

Whipped cream, for serving (optional)

1. Preheat the oven to 350°F. Grease a 9-inch round springform pan with butter.

2. Halve the plums and discard the pits. If the plums are big, you can cut them into fourths; otherwise go with halves. Set them aside.

3. In the bowl of a stand mixer fitted with the paddle attachment, combine 8 tablespoons (1 stick) of butter and ½ cup of sugar and beat on medium speed for about 5 minutes, scraping down the sides of the bowl as needed, until light and fluffy. Add the lemon zest and beat until combined. Add the eggs, one at a time, beating and scraping the bowl after each addition.

4. In another bowl, mix together 1½ cups of flour and the baking powder. Add the flour mixture to the mixer and beat until smooth.

5. Spread the batter evenly into the prepared pan. Sprinkle the dough evenly with 1 tablespoon of vanilla pudding powder. Layer the plums onto the batter so that they're overlapping. Sprinkle them with the remaining 1 tablespoon of vanilla pudding powder.

6. Cut the remaining 4 tablespoons (½ stick) of butter into small cubes. In a bowl, combine the remaining 1 cup of flour and the remaining ¼ cup of sugar. To make the streusel topping, add the butter cubes and rub the butter and flour mixture between your fingers until it's a mixture of small and large crumbs. Distribute the streusel evenly over the plums.

7. Bake for 50 to 55 minutes, or until a toothpick inserted into the center comes out clean. Let cool on a cooling rack. Serve with whipped cream (if using).

INGREDIENT TIP: Use Italian prune plums if you can find them. If not, any plums will do. If the fruit is particularly squishy, sprinkle a little cornstarch or extra vanilla pudding powder on the batter before topping it with the plums.

VARIATION TIP: Try apricots or peaches instead of plums.

LIGHTNING CAKE
Blitztorte

Serves 12 | **Prep time:** 30 minutes | **Cook time:** 20 minutes, plus 1 hour to cool

VEGETARIAN

"Blitz" means lightning, and the idea is that a Blitztorte is lightning fast to make, at least in baking terms. It's a great recipe to have in your arsenal. It looks fancy but doesn't really require too many special skills. This recipe comes from my Tante (aunt), who makes it with gooseberries, my favorite, but since they can be scarce in my part of the world, I use raspberries or even canned cherries.

8 tablespoons (1 stick) butter, plus more for greasing the pans

1 cup granulated sugar, divided

1 teaspoon vanilla extract

4 eggs, separated

1¼ cups all-purpose flour

1 teaspoon baking powder

6 tablespoons milk

½ cup sliced almonds

2 cups heavy (whipping) cream

2 teaspoons powdered sugar

2 cups fresh raspberries, gooseberries, canned cherries, or other berries

1. Preheat the oven to 350°F. Grease 2 (9-inch) springform pans with butter and cover the bottom of the pans with parchment paper.

2. In a stand mixer fitted with the paddle attachment, combine the butter and ½ cup of granulated sugar and beat on medium speed for 4 to 5 minutes until light and fluffy. Add the vanilla and egg yolks and beat, scraping down the bowl as needed, until combined.

3. In a small bowl, mix together the flour and baking powder, then add it to the mixer, alternating with the milk, and beat until combined. Press half of the batter into each prepared springform pan. Set aside.

4. In a super-clean mixing bowl, using the whisk attachment, whip the egg whites, slowly adding the remaining ½ cup of granulated sugar. Continue whipping until stiff peaks form (you should be able to see the slash mark if you draw a knife through the meringue).

5. Spread half of the meringue into each springform pan, spreading it to the edge. Sprinkle half of the almonds over the meringue in each pan.

6. Bake for 20 minutes. Let the cakes cool completely on a cooling rack.

7. When the cakes are completely cool, run a knife carefully around the edge to loosen any stuck meringue, remove the rings of the springform pans, and remove the cakes from the bases.

8. In a stand mixer fitted with the whisk attachment, whip the cream for 30 seconds, add the powdered sugar, and continue to whip until stiff peaks form.

9. Place the less attractive cake on a serving platter and put the springform ring around the cake to act as a guide. Cover the cake with the berries almost to the edge. Cover the berries with the whipped cream. Place the second cake over the whipped cream, pressing down a little to make sure it's all together. Remove the ring, cut into slices, and serve.

BLACK FOREST CHERRY CAKE
Schwarzwälder Kirschtorte

Serves 12 | **Prep time:** 25 minutes | **Cook time:** 1 hour,
plus 6 hours to rest and decorate

VEGETARIAN

My daughter fell in love with this classic cake on a trip to Germany and requests it for her birthday every year. The whipped cream, dark chocolate, and cherries of this cake represent the Tracht, *or regional dress, of the Black Forest—white stockings, dark dress, and a hat with bright red balls on top.*

Nonstick cooking spray

1 ounce unsweetened chocolate

4 tablespoons (½ stick) butter

6 eggs, separated

1 cup granulated sugar

1½ cups all-purpose flour

½ cup unsweetened cocoa powder

2 teaspoons baking powder

Pinch salt

1 jar Morello cherries

2 tablespoons cornstarch

4 tablespoons kirsch or cherry juice, divided

4 cups heavy (whipping) cream

¼ cup powdered sugar

1 milk or dark chocolate bar, for decorating

12 fresh cherries, for decorating (optional)

1. Preheat the oven to 350°F. Spray a 9-inch springform pan with cooking spray and line the bottom with parchment paper.

2. In a microwave-safe bowl, microwave the unsweetened chocolate and butter at 50 percent power for 1 minute, stir, and repeat until melted. Stir until combined. Set aside to cool.

3. Using a stand mixer fitted with the whisk attachment, beat the egg whites to stiff peaks, then transfer them to a medium bowl and set aside. Add the egg yolks, granulated sugar, and the cooled butter and chocolate mixture to the mixer bowl and beat until frothy.

4. In a medium bowl, mix together the flour, cocoa powder, baking powder, and salt. Sift the mixture into the egg yolk mixture and fold until combined.

5. Add the beaten egg whites and carefully fold them into the batter in batches, until there are no streaks of white left.

6. Pour the batter into the prepared cake pan and bake for 45 minutes, or until a toothpick inserted into the center comes out clean. Let cool on a cooling rack for 20 minutes.

7. Using a knife, loosen the cake around the sides, then release the spring-form ring and let the cake cool completely, 2 to 3 hours.

8. Strain the Morello cherries from the juice, reserving both. In a medium saucepan, whisk together the strained cherry juice and cornstarch and slowly bring to a boil over medium heat. When the mixture is thickened, add the Morello cherries, stir until combined, and remove from the heat. Add 1 tablespoon of kirsch and stir. Pour the cherry filling into a bowl to cool.

9. Using a stand mixer fitted with the whisk attachment, whip the cream on high speed, add the powdered sugar, and continue whipping until it holds stiff peaks. Set aside 1 cup for decoration.

10. Cut the cooled cake horizontally into 3 even layers. Place one layer on a serving platter. Sprinkle the cake layer with 1 or 2 tablespoons of kirsch, spread half of the cherry filling over it, and 1 cup of whipped cream. Add the second layer of cake and repeat the process. Top with the final layer of cake.

11. Using an offset spatula, spread the reserved whipped cream over the sides and top of the cake.

12. Using a vegetable peeler, shave the chocolate bar over the cake. Arrange the fresh cherries (if using) around the edge of the cake. Refrigerate the cake until ready to serve.

GINGERBREAD BARS
Lebkuchen vom Blech

Makes 20 cookies | **Prep time:** 25 minutes | **Cook time:** 35 minutes

VEGETARIAN

Lebkuchen recipes date back to the 1300s, when traders started bringing exotic spices to Germany that were used to make long-lasting gingerbread for travelers. This recipe features a simple glaze, but the bars can be decorated with candied citrus or blanched almonds as well.

FOR THE SPICE MIX

2½ teaspoons ground cinnamon

2 teaspoons ground cloves

½ teaspoon ground cardamom

½ teaspoon ground ginger

½ teaspoon ground coriander

½ teaspoon ground aniseed

¼ teaspoon ground allspice

¼ teaspoon ground nutmeg

FOR THE COOKIES

4 cups all-purpose flour

2 teaspoons baking powder

1¼ cups granulated sugar

1 cup ground almonds

10 tablespoons plus 2 teaspoons (1¼ sticks plus 2 teaspoons) butter, at room temperature

½ cup strong brewed coffee, at room temperature

2 eggs

1 tablespoon rum

3 tablespoons unsweetened cocoa powder

½ teaspoon salt

1 cup honey, warmed

1½ cups powdered sugar (optional)

3 to 4 tablespoons water (optional)

TO MAKE THE SPICE MIX

1. In a small bowl, mix together the cinnamon, cloves, cardamom, ginger, coriander, aniseed, allspice, and nutmeg. Set aside.

TO MAKE THE COOKIES

2. Preheat the oven to 350°F. Line a 9-by-13-inch baking pan with parchment paper.

3. In the bowl of a stand mixer fitted with the paddle attachment, combine the flour, baking powder, granulated sugar, almonds, butter, coffee, eggs, rum, cocoa powder, salt, honey, and the spice mix and beat on medium speed until smooth.

4. Pour the batter into the prepared pan and smooth the top.

5. Bake for 30 to 35 minutes until a toothpick inserted into the center comes out clean. Let cool for a few minutes on a wire rack.

6. If you want to glaze the bars, in a small bowl, mix together the powdered sugar and 3 tablespoons of water until smooth (if it's too thick, add the remaining 1 tablespoon of water). Spread the glaze over the warm lebkuchen. Let cool completely, cut into pieces, and serve.

RUM BALLS
Rumkugeln

Makes 30 to 40 balls | **Prep time:** 40 minutes, plus 30 minutes to chill

NO-COOK · VEGETARIAN

As a child, I was convinced rum balls were a super sophisticated, adults-only treat: rich, smooth chocolate truffles with just a hint of rum, rolled in cocoa powder or chocolate sprinkles, depending on whether you like bitter or sweet. Go ahead and tell the kids they are for grown-ups, so you can keep them for yourself. I won't tell. You can make them look fancy by serving them in mini-cupcake liners.

7 ounces semisweet chocolate

3½ ounces dark chocolate

8 tablespoons (1 stick) butter, at room temperature

¾ cup powdered sugar

4 tablespoons dark rum

½ cup unsweetened cocoa powder, or ¾ cup chocolate sprinkles, for coating the rum balls

1. Place the semisweet chocolate and dark chocolate in a microwave-safe bowl or measuring cup. Microwave at 50 percent power for 1 minute, stir, and repeat until melted. Stir until combined. Set aside to cool.

2. In a stand mixer fitted with the paddle attachment, beat the butter for 4 to 5 minutes until light and fluffy. Sift the powdered sugar into the butter and beat for 3 to 4 minutes, scraping down the bowl as needed, until fluffy.

3. When the melted chocolate is cooled to room temperature, add it to the butter and sugar mixture. Add the rum and beat, scraping down the sides as needed, until smooth. Cover the bowl and refrigerate for 30 minutes.

4. Set up a workstation. Line a baking sheet with wax paper. Put the cocoa powder into a small bowl. Set the bowl of chilled chocolate in the work area.

5. Using a melon baller or a spoon, scoop the chocolate into walnut-size balls and roll them with your clean hands to make them round. Drop the balls into the cocoa powder and toss them around to coat. Place the coated balls on the wax paper. Repeat with the remaining chocolate mixture.

6. The balls can be stored in an airtight container between layers of wax paper at room temperature for up to a week.

COOKING TIP: When rolling the balls, make sure your hands are clean and a bit cool. If the chocolate starts to stick to your hands, wash your hands with cold water. You can also dust your hands with cocoa powder, which should help stop the sticking.

VANILLA CRESCENTS
Vanillekipferl

Makes 45 to 50 cookies | **Prep time:** 1 hour, plus 30 minutes to chill
Cook time: 30 minutes

VEGETARIAN

Vanilla crescent cookies originated in Austria, where they were created to celebrate a victory over Turkey. (Can you just see it? "We won the war! Let's bake cookies!") Today, they might be a beloved Christmas cookie, but I think they are perfect at any time of year. The rich and delicate cookies are loaded with almond flavor and get their sweetness from a coating of sugar. Bake a batch to enjoy with a cup of coffee.

1½ cups all-purpose flour
1 egg yolk
2 teaspoons vanilla extract

¾ cup powdered sugar
1 cup ground almonds

1 cup (2 sticks) cold
   butter, cubed
½ cup granulated sugar

1. In a food processor, combine the flour, egg yolk, vanilla, powdered sugar, and ground almonds and pulse until combined. Add the butter cubes one at a time, pulsing until each is incorporated and the mixture forms a dough.

2. Lay a piece of plastic wrap on the counter and place the dough on top. Use the plastic to help shape the dough into a log, about 2 inches in diameter. Wrap the log tightly in the plastic wrap, squeezing and forming as you go. Refrigerate for 30 minutes.

3. Preheat the oven to 350°F. Line 2 baking sheets with parchment paper.

4. Put the granulated sugar in a small bowl and set aside.

5. Cut a ¼- to ½-inch slice of dough and roll it between your hands into a mini log shape. Taper the ends, bend the dough to form a crescent shape, and place it on the prepared baking sheet. Repeat with the rest of the dough, spacing the cookies about 1 inch apart. Bake each baking sheet, one at a time, for 12 minutes, or until the cookies start browning around the edges.

6. Place the baking sheets on a cooling rack. Take a warm cookie and roll it in the sugar. Return the cookie to the cooling rack to cool and repeat with the rest of the cookies.

LEFTOVERS TIP: These cookies are fragile, but they can be stored at room temperature in a plastic airtight container layered with wax paper for up to 2 months.

GERMAN ICED COFFEE
Eiskaffee

Serves 4 | **Prep time:** 20 minutes

5-INGREDIENT · 30-MINUTE · NO-COOK · ONE-POT · VEGETARIAN

When you order an Eiskaffee in Germany, you don't get a glass of cold coffee with ice cubes in it. Rather, you'll be lucky enough to indulge in a decadent dessert with ice cream, whipped cream, chocolate, and, of course, coffee. It's the kind of dessert you order in an outdoor café on a warm afternoon to enjoy while watching the world go by. Fortunately, it's easy enough to make at home.

1 cup heavy (whipping) cream

4 cups brewed coffee, at room temperature

4 cups vanilla ice cream

1 milk chocolate bar

Waffle cookies, for serving

1. In a stand mixer fitted with the whisk attachment, whip the cream until it holds stiff peaks.

2. Pour 1 cup of coffee into each of 4 tall glasses or goblets. Add 1 cup of ice cream and a quarter of the whipped cream to each glass.

3. Using a vegetable peeler, shave the chocolate bar over each glass. Serve with a waffle cookie.

RESOURCES

Books

Ursula Heinzelmann. *Beyond Bratwurst: A History of Food in Germany*.
London: Reaktion Books, 2014.
A fascinating look at the history of Germany's food from the very beginning,
including regional differences and outside influences.

Dr. Oetker Schulkochbuch. Bielefeld: Dr. Oetker, 1984.
This "school cookbook" is the basic cooking primer and reference for German
food. My copy is well worn.

Culinaria Germany. Edited by Christine Metzger. Cologne: Könemann, 2000.
An overview of German regional cooking with a deep dive into specific
ingredients.

Websites

GermanGirlinAmerica.com
My website, loaded with recipes, as well as posts about holidays, travel, history, literature, and German products.

AllTastesGerman.com
Angela Schofield's fantastic site with great German recipes and video
instruction.

SpoonfulsofGermany.com
A look at German food in all its diversity with wonderful stories from Nadia
Hassani.

Quick-German-Recipes.com
Traditional German recipes from Canadian blogger Gerhild Fulson.

German Food Sources

GermanGirlinAmerica.com
Find an index of German restaurants, bakeries, and delis, organized by state and city, on the home page of the site. You'll also find a list of great sources to order German foods online.

GermanShop24.com
My go-to for German products. They carry sweets, seasonings, bread, holiday goods, coffee, and chocolate, shipped to you from Germany.

BavariaSausage.com
Aufschnitt and sausages made fresh in Wisconsin.

INDEX

Acknowledgments

There are many people who inspired me and encouraged me as I wrote this book. First, thank you to my mother, my Tanten, and my Oma, for letting me hang out in the kitchen and for teaching me so much about German food. You set a high bar, and I hope I made you all proud. Thank you to Kevin, my Tech Guy, who gave me the courage to start writing, and who continues to give me support and encouragement every day. K&K.

I also want to thank Nadia Hassani from Spoonfuls of Germany, Dale Blank of the Freistadt Alte Kameraden, Angela Schofield from All Tastes German, Gerhild Fulson from Just Like Oma, and Susanne Bacon, author of the Wycliff novels. Each of you is talented and supportive, and I might have given up long ago without your words of encouragement. Thanks also to all of my editors who reminded me that brevity is a good thing!

Finally, *vielen Dank* to all of you who connect with the words on my website. We really are one big German-American club. Let's all get together for a kaffeeklatsch next week!

About the Author

 **KAREN LODDER** is a writer and the creator of GermanGirlinAmerica.com. Her parents immigrated to America shortly before she was born, so she grew up in a Southern California home where the food and culture were all German. Summer visits to family in Germany reinforced her love for the country but especially for the food. One of Karen's favorite memories is of sitting on the kitchen counter watching how her Oma prepared amazing meals with simple ingredients. Watching and tasting led to cooking and then sharing her favorite recipes and memories of growing up German in America. You can follow her @germangirlinamerica on Facebook and Instagram.